Look at what others are saying about
The Intrepid Way!

Wes Weaver
Real Estate Investor
Streamline International, Inc.
Columbus, GA

Knowing and working with Matthew has been a true inspiration that has changed my life. He has been the fuel that has sustained my entrepreneurial flame for the last few years now. He opened up my mind to The Intrepid Way lifestyle that I never knew existed. I was 22-years old looking forward to being 65 so I could finally retire like all the other people I worked with. Two years and many real estate transactions later, using the principles of The Intrepid Way, I am unemployable and looking to bring retirement a lot closer. Matthew has shown me the power of income layers and how it could buy me the most precious thing money could buy and that was my personal time!

If you're ready for paradigm shifts, read this book! In his book The Intrepid Way, Matthew stresses the importance of creating goodwill in business and continues to walk his talk by using his excellent skills to empower others. I'm always looking for new ideas, new distinctions, and different ways of looking at familiar concepts. If you are too, then I highly recommend The Intrepid Way. Read the book if you want to grow your business and deepen your financial education! Your mind will thank you!

Will Brooks
Business Entrepreneur
Fayetteville, NC

Marleen Geyen
President
The Geyen Group, Inc
Minneapolis, MN

Is "The Intrepid Way" for you? I have known Matthew for several years and this book speaks volumes about the passion he has for others to live a life of Personal Freedom. It is a **must read** for anyone interested in challenging their beliefs and emotions with unconventional wisdom. Matthew leads the way for anyone to have the Time Freedom and Monetary Freedom they desire. Thank you Matthew!

I have known Matthew Chan for several years and the words I use to describe him are integrity, generous, energetic, and brilliant. The Intrepid Way has been a labor of love for him so that he can give the world a gift that will last a lifetime. He shares the story of his journey to Personal Freedom with hopes that others will be inspired to stop living a life of mediocrity. We all know how important a strong foundation is for the integrity of a building. In The Intrepid Way philosophy, Matthew shares his Money Layers concept as the way to build a strong financial foundation to reach Personal Freedom. Thank you Matthew, you truly make a difference in this world.

Cindy Chapin
Event Promotions
Destiny Creations
ccdestinycreations.com
Glendale, AZ

Melita Hunt
Senior Executive
IITM, Inc
www.iitm.com
Cary, NC

Finally, a book that gets to the heart of the matter! If you aren't living the life of your dreams or reaching your goals, then who is responsible for making it happen? Only you! Clear and easy to understand, The Intrepid Way outlines the choices Matthew made and lessons he learned on the road to Personal Freedom. He shares his knowledge with you as a guide for anyone who is willing to step up to the plate and be responsible for designing their own life - the way that they want it to look!

Writing from his heart while allowing his voice to be heard, Matthew has constructed a candid, on point, and insightful guide that will help you to realize that there is a better way – an Intrepid Way that will allow you to obtain a life of true personal freedom. Matthew's real-life experiences, struggles, and triumphs set an example that will empower and encourage you to follow your heart, make your own choices, and create the life of abundance you not only desire but deserve. Beyond financial freedom, Matthew will inspire you to create your most valuable asset – TIME FREEDOM. Matthew courageously expresses truths that some could construe as controversial. Perhaps that is why this is appropriately called, "The Intrepid Way".

Stephanie Olsen
Advanced Financial
Strategist
The Ark Inc.
www.thearkinc.com
Reno, NV

Christi Williams
Real Estate
Entrepreneur
StrongWills, Inc.
Houston, TX

The Intrepid Way is a must read! I loved every chapter! Last night after the children were in bed, the one powerful lesson I learned from the book is the attainment of personal freedom. I loved it because many, many books out there will tell you all about financial freedom and how to gain that, but yours is the first to uncover the hidden motive behind most people's drive for financial freedom in the first place… the attainment of true personal freedom.

Matthew has such a gift for saying things in a relevant, easy to understand manner. Whether you are currently an active entrepreneur or just beginning your journey to discover the entrepreneurial spirit that lies within yourself, The Intrepid Way is for you!

In The Intrepid Way, Matthew lays down the realities of true freedom and the price one must pay to reach it. He describes the required shift to "unconventional thinking" to achieve ultimate freedom. Page after page, he takes us through many of the thoughts and illusions we don't even realize are swimming through our minds and contaminating our lives.

In today's society, people have been misled by "teachers" without real wisdom; down a path where they expect to be bailed out later in life by the government. Matthew describes how people are living on their own Titanic; stuck on a sinking ship, paralyzed as it goes down, believing they have no options. The Intrepid Way lays out honest truth and sheds light on what it takes to be truly free.

I highly endorse and recommend this powerful, hard-hitting display of printed truth for anyone seeking guidance to personal freedom.

Damion Lupo
President & CEO
Denali Investment
Group, Inc.
www.cashtruck.com
Scottsdale, AZ

Matthew Chan has given us a brilliant blueprint for a life worth living. The Intrepid Way provokes, inspires, and challenges us to truthfully examine our often-times unexamined life. He demonstrates through his own personal experience, keen intuitive insights, and observations how each of us can attain the greatest of freedoms with the greatest efficiency: personal freedom, financial freedom, spiritual freedom, and the most precious of all, time freedom. Matthew is a man who boldly walks his talk. Whether you're hungry for subtle distinctions or massive change in your life, do yourself a favor and devour this book. The Intrepid Way is a true gift to the world.

Dean Edelson
President
*Elysium
Investment Group
www.eighomes.com
Sedona, AZ*

Troy Arment
Real Estate
Entrepreneur
*Mid-Continent
Funding Group,
Inc.
Wichita, KS*

Superb, thought-provoking! Matthew challenges conventional wisdom as only he can. By giving us a peek into his own personal challenges, trials, and triumphs, Matthew allows us a rare look into what it takes to live a life being true to yourself and following your dreams.

However, I feel the greatest gift he has given in this book is the gift of his psychology. Chapter 6 of this book is worth the price of the book alone. Incorporating these principles has helped my business more than anything else I have done. The Intrepid Way gives you all the tools to begin the journey of living the life you only dreamed was possible before.

Before reading The Intrepid Way, I was on the path to becoming a lemming-like employee. But after reading the book, I "unplugged" myself from the employee mentality. As a young adult, I now realize there are multiple paths to creating my future. The Intrepid Way has opened my eyes to opportunities I have never seen before and given me the ability to face adversity with faith. I have become more responsible than ever before. By embracing my entrepreneurial spirit, my soul has been energized to achieve personal freedom.

Paolo Bruno
Entrepreneur
Orlando, FL

The Intrepid Way

How to Create the Freedom You Need to Live the Life You Want!

Matthew S. Chan

Ascend Beyond Publishing
Columbus, Georgia

The Intrepid Way
How to Create the Freedom You Need to Live the Life You Want!

Copyright © 2004 by Matthew S. Chan. All rights reserved.

"The Intrepid Way" is a trademark of Intrepid Network Concepts, Inc.

Published by: Ascend Beyond Publishing
                 5435 Woodruff Farm Rd., #B-300
                 PMB 158
                 Columbus, GA 31907

ISBN: 0-9713947-7-6

Printed in the United States of America. First Edition.

First Printing: January 2004

Book Ordering Information
Visit our website at www.theintrepidway.com to order additional copies for private use, or for resale. Quantity discounts are available. Special pricing for churches, schools, colleges, universities, and non-profit, charitable organizations.

Visit our website at **www.theintrepidway.com** to find more information on books, educational materials, and courses to create your personal freedom.

Dedication

To the people who believed and trusted in me in this journey...

To the people who helped me get to where I dreamed of ...

To the people who are sick of the daily grind and want to make a change ...

To the people who want a fresh new start and willing to make it happen ....

To the people who believe there is another way to work and live ...

To the people who want to awaken the entrepreneurial genius within them...

I commit this book to them. Salute.

Matthew S. Chan

Table of Contents

3 Financial Principles

4 The Work Principles

5

Entrepreneurial Mindset

6

Personal Support Networks

7

Business Networks

8

Education & Learning

In Conclusion

Introduction

In the Spring of 2002, I realized that I was going to hit a significant milestone in my life. That milestone was that I would not have to work everyday to maintain my lifestyle. In fact, I could get away with putting in only a few hours a day and then I could kick back, relax, and watch TV for the next few years.

It didn't mean I became suddenly rich or anything. Nor did it mean that I didn't have to lift a finger to do any work. It simply meant that I had enough streaming income to support my middle-class lifestyle to take two weeks off nearly anytime I wanted to.

And you know what? I did. I did enjoy taking some time off doing what I wanted to do such as reading, talking to people, travel, and basically lounged around a bit. But anyone who knows me knows that I don't stay still for long. I like having some excitement in my life. I like learning new things, meeting new people, and taking on new challenges.

For years, I thought about writing a book but I never felt qualified to write about anything that I was passionate about. After all, writing a book which no one is interested in reading is mostly the job for a college textbook writer.

Having written small articles and small story pieces over the years, I accumulated two thick notebooks full of written material on opinions I had on different subjects.

One night in Atlanta, I was in a friend's apartment. We were sharing our thoughts and dreams of the future. Specifically, I told him one day I wanted to write a book but I really did not know what my message was going to be. He shared with me an insight that caused a chain of events that has resulted in this book.

And what he told me was this ... "Matthew, what you have accomplished for yourself and the life you lead, I wish I could do it. I would be so happy if I could be in your position."

At first, I dismissed it. Then I thought about it. And then he explained, "So many people like me are trapped in their jobs and don't know how to leave to support ourselves. We don't know what it takes. Yes, I could become a self-employed programmer but how do I be self-employed without having to work to death and be certain that the income will continue. And if I stop working or I can't find an assignment, I won't have any money."

After a pause, he continued, "At least being an employee, I have some assurances that my income will continue. And yet, I know I am trapped and it is not where I want to be. I want to be free to spend my time to do what I want and when I want to like you do. I am tired of working with people I don't like."

Ironically, a year earlier, I had a conversation with another friend that also said that he wanted to live my lifestyle.

In both cases, they knew I was not rich, nor was I living high on the hog. I simply lived a fairly middle-class life from a material point of view. Yet, from a lifestyle point of view, I was going to different places meeting different people working on interesting projects spending time on things that mattered to me working largely on my own timetable.

I had the monetary freedom and time freedom to do so.

In retrospect, I suppose I took it all for granted. Because the fact was, many friends I have throughout the U.S. live a similar lifestyle as I do. In many cases, I thought they did even better than me. So I did not think what I did was anything special, nor anything especially incredible. I was simply living my life primarily the way I wanted to.

But today when I pause and look around, I do find that most people have a ton of responsibilities they have taken on because they have few apparent options.

And part of that is getting up early and going to work everyday to a job they dislike. Most do it because they have to. And even if they wanted to stop, they don't feel like they can. They have no idea how to move on to something new. The only refuge they have are their weekends, holidays, and vacation time.

For me, it might as well have been another lifetime ago. It has been so many years ago since I had to worry about a job that it is foreign to me. And yet there it is around me, all around me, unhappy people spending their lives doing things they don't want to do until old age.

When these separate insights came together, I understood what I needed and wanted to write about. It was about achieving personal freedom. I know many people who have achieved what I have achieved and more but few really talk about how they did it and what they went through. Similar to what I originally thought, they don't consider what they have done to be especially notable. I have since realized, it is all in the eye of the beholder.

Because I had the good fortune to meet two people who made me see, truly see what I had, I then felt comfortable enough and "qualified" enough to undertake the task to write this book. But what a fun task it has been going down memory lane to explore the events in my own life that I thought might benefit you. In some cases, it made me happy. In other cases, it made me sad. Either way, it has helped shape the person I am today and the lessons I am about to share with you within this book.

I hope you don't make the same mistakes I made. And I hope you experience successes quicker than I did. If this book helped you see things a little differently, sidestep some potential pitfalls, or overcome some personal challenges, I will have taken great satisfaction in completing this book.

Thank you for reading my book. I hope one day we can meet.

Matthew S. Chan

The Intrepid Way

1 | The Intrepid Way Philosophy

Personal Freedom

So what is personal freedom? Well ... personal freedom is actually a pretty broad term. It can mean freedom of speech, freedom to practice your religion, freedom to travel, freedom to bear arms, and so on. However, this book is not quite as ambitious to deal with more constitutional, political, or religious issues.

In the context of this book, my definition of personal freedom is a simple formula:

PERSONAL FREEDOM = MONETARY FREEDOM + TIME FREEDOM

During my own journey towards personal freedom, I thought I had achieved it *twice*. But unfortunately both of those times were only temporary and mere illusions. The first time I tried to create personal freedom ... I did so knowingly sacrificing the monetary freedom part of the equation. The second time, I thought I had indeed created monetary freedom ... but as I said that was only an illusion. However, this time around I believe I finally have it right.

1

The reason I believe this is because I had many teachers to learn from ... and I have numerous friends who either share my position or are in fact better position.

I see many people who may have either time freedom or monetary freedom ... but it seems that not too many have *both*.

There are some people who have achieved monetary freedom, but they don't necessarily have the time freedom to enjoy it. For example: one of my relatives, who has worked all her life to create wealth and ongoing income for her family, has in fact achieved this goal. But she is afraid to let go because she feels that no one else can manage her assets and business affairs better than what she can. She believes that she cannot "afford" help. Therefore, because of this attitude, she has little time to enjoy all that she has created.

There are also those people who have time freedom, but they cannot truly enjoy it without the financial means to indulge in it. An example of this would be people I've seen living in low-income neighborhoods; who sit on a porch all day or simply walk the streets because they have too much time on their hands. But you see ... they also don't have the financial means to enjoy the abundance of time that they have.

In my experience, there is no personal freedom if you have no time freedom. You also do not have personal freedom if you do not have some degree of monetary freedom. *You must have both*.

The journey to creating personal freedom is a *lifestyle choice* that nearly *anyone* can enjoy today. And it can improve year after year. I have found that creating personal freedom is actually quite simple ... but it does require discipline, commitment, passion, and most importantly - personal growth.

A lot of people think it's more important to look rich than it is for them to be personally free. I know this because I see plenty of affluent people who look good - but then complain that they don't have enough time to relax or enjoy the much simpler things in life.

Further still, if they were to stop working, they would most certainly (and rather quickly) lose their lifestyles. If those people had more time and could stop working as hard, they would be so much happier. These people wish that they were rich ... but the reality of it is that having personal freedom does not require them to be rich.

However, there is some good news! When you do become personally free, you can either stop where you are and enjoy your current lifestyle, or you can continue on to become rich ... where you are personally free, but continuously improving your lifestyle along the way.

Maintain Your Freedom

Most people know that American citizens are among the freest people in the world. We certainly have a lot of civic and religious freedom. However, this is a freedom that has been hard-fought for by many generations of Americans and early immigrants. I feel that too many people take their civic freedoms for granted ... while there are others who are committed to fighting for it and preserving it.

There are many countries where civic and religious freedoms are still being fought for ... and many of these countries have citizens literally dreaming about being free.

As an American citizen, I publicly acknowledge the people in the armed forces. They protect our country from invaders or terrorists who would seek to destroy it ... along with all of the freedoms we enjoy today.

I traveled by airplane quite frequently before the terrorist attack on September 11, 2001. Actually, I still do! However, I have noticed that while I may still be considered a free citizen of the United States, I truly do not have that much freedom when I decide to travel by plane. Also, what few freedoms I had in the airport or in an airplane prior to September 11, 2001 have now been diminished even further.

I recently flew out to California to spend a long weekend with some friends of mine. After checking in and reaching the security post, I had to put my bag through the scanners ... along with my watch, cell phone, and notebook computer. I emptied my pockets of all coins ... and even took my belt buckle off. Yet ... I still triggered the alarm!

In turn, I was subjected to a complete body search. However, it turned out that it was the hidden metal wires lining my shoes that triggered the alarm.

The point I am trying to make here is that not only do I have to worry about what I pack, but now I also have to worry about the clothing I wear. If I don't ... then my freedom becomes diminished - because they will pull me to the side and search me.

I understand why it has to be done, and I am always polite and cooperative during the entire process. But I have no false notions that I am completely free once I enter an airport. In fact, I have even less freedom when I board an airplane.

Freedom can be given ... but freedom can also be taken away. In order for freedom to be preserved, it *must* be maintained. For example, we maintain our civic freedom by paying taxes to subsidize our police and armed forces. If we don't, we may find terrorists or other foreign invaders trying to take away all the freedoms that were bravely fought for throughout the last 250 years.

All American citizens are born with civic freedoms. This has been ensured by the Constitution of the United States, the Bill of Rights, and other U.S. Laws. Americans are not born with their freedoms taken from them ... they are born *given* to them by our government. All of us must accept the responsibility to behave accordingly in order to maintain our civic freedoms.

Thousands of people across the country go to jail every day. Their civic freedoms have been taken from them as punishment for crimes they committed. Some only stay in jail a few days, while many others are there for the rest of their lives.

If someone is convicted of a crime and goes to prison, they have lost their civic freedom. Of course with the exception of the most heinous of offenses, the prisoner will one day regain most of their civic freedom. Civic freedom will be granted as long as a citizen continues to behave responsibly.

At this point you may be asking yourself, "What does all of this have to do with personal freedom?"

There are people who are born into monetary freedom by virtue of their families. These people are what I call, "Members of The Lucky Genes Club." They were born into wealth, and the wealth is maintained by the infrastructure set up by their families.

However, there are many more of us who were not born into monetary freedom. We have to create it, earn it, and then maintain it. Much like civic freedom, monetary freedom can be gained or lost. It all depends on the actions you take, how responsible you are, and how well you can preserve and maintain it.

Because most people have never attained any degree of personal freedom, they cannot make the distinction that it can also be lost. They think it is a one-way trip. But surprise! It's not!

There are varying degrees of monetary freedom:

- You can be free and be rich.

- You can be free and not be rich.

- You can be rich and not be free.

- You can be not rich and be not free.

I am sure it is no surprise to you that most people fall within that last statement.

As I said, being rich can help you be monetarily free ... but it certainly isn't a guarantee.

What is Wealth & Monetary Freedom?

So what is monetary freedom if it is not being rich?

My teachers talked about an inventor/genius they studied under. His name is R. Buckminster Fuller ... or "Bucky" to his friends and acquaintances. One of the last books he wrote before he died was entitled, "Critical Path." In this book, Fuller provided his definition of real wealth in Chapter 6, page 199.

It is a passage you could read it six times and still not fully understand it. There are many granularities and distinctions to what Fuller considered as real wealth.

However, I have taken the liberty to use much simpler terms that most of us can relate to:

Real wealth is measured by your ability to create sufficient, ongoing income, so that you can support your current (or preferred) standard of living for yourself (and your family) for so many days forward, so that you have the time and means to live the life you want without substantially working.

For example, if your current standard of living is $5,000 per month, and you make $5,000 per month in your job, you wealth is zero. Although you are making enough to support yourself, you have to "substantially work" to earn that. If you "substantially" stopped working, you would probably be fired from your job ... and thus you would not be able to support yourself.

Let's say you saved up $10,000 and your current standard of living is still $5,000 per month. If you "substantially" stopped working and got fired, then according to Fuller's definition of wealth, you would have two months of wealth. If you saved $100,000 ... assuming no inflation ... you would have twenty months (a little over 1.5 years) of wealth. If you saved $1 million ... again assuming no inflation ... you would have 200 months (over 16.5 years) of wealth.

Let's say you had income from businesses or investments (that you didn't have to "substantially" work in every day) of $6,000 per month, and your standard of living was $5,000 per month. You would potentially have an infinite amount of wealth. You could live "forever" as long as the businesses and investments were well maintained and managed. $6,000 per month obviously does not qualify you as being rich ... but as you can see, you can be "perpetually wealthy" without being rich.

When you become "perpetually wealthy," you then achieve monetary freedom.

Monetary Freedom = "Perpetual Wealth"

Monetary freedom is when you are able to financially support your current standard of living without having to substantially work.

You may be asking yourself why I didn't use the phrase, "Monetary freedom is when you are able to financially support your current standard of living with *no work*."

I say, "without having to substantially work" versus "with no work" because the notion of "no work" is largely a fairy tale for the types of people who pin all their hopes on great inheritances, lottery tickets, or get-rich-quick schemes. It could happen for a lucky few ... but for most of us, that is not a very likely or rewarding plan to base your financial future on.

Anyone in a position of responsibility, such as a successful business owner, manager, or investor, will have to expend some amount of personal energy in overseeing his or her businesses, finances, and investments.

Even a person of great wealth who hires employees, property managers, financial managers, investment brokers, and accountants to do all the managerial and detail work must expend some small amount of personal time and energy (work). For example, to have a conversation with one of them to receive a status report. It may only be ten minutes per person, but he would have "worked." Even if he spent five minutes to open an envelope and look at an investment statement or log in to check the status of his portfolio, he *still* would have "worked" but it does not mean he *substantially* worked.

The only time when "no work" occurs is when ALL responsibility has been absolved to someone else. This could happen with minor children, invalids, or of course those members of "The Lucky Genes Club." But for the rest of us, one of the assumptions in this book is that WE are responsible for creating and intelligently maintaining and preserving our monetary freedom. The price of not learning reminds me of a famous saying I have taken creative liberties with:

"A fool and his money will ALWAYS be parted."

Substantially Working

What is "substantially working"?

In being a full-time employee or a self-employed worker, you are substantially working. During my ten years in the corporate world, being a full-time employee meant working anywhere between 40 and 60 hours a week. There was never any question in my mind whether I had to substantially work. I did. I know because I would be mentally or physically worn out by the end of the day. And let me tell you, I truly enjoyed my weekends, holidays, and vacations. I had to! It was the only time I could call my own!

Even when I was a contract instructor and worked as little as one week a month to maintain my standard of living, I still felt like I had to substantially work. I didn't work as hard as I did as an employee and I had more free time, but I still substantially worked because during my "off periods" I would be actively reading and

8

studying so that I could maintain my cutting-edge status.

But I also realized that if I stopped taking assignments, my income would immediately stop.

Today, I have little need to substantially work to maintain my standard of living. I continue to actively work because I wish to continue on improving my lifestyle and to one day become rich. I have set up my affairs so that if I suddenly stopped working ... my income WILL NOT suddenly stop.

I would like to emphasize that when you don't have to substantially work, you have the time freedom to do what you want ... when you want.

As I see it, with the exception of top management personnel at large companies, most employees and self-employed workers are not monetarily free ... and nowhere close to it. Employees may attain monetary freedom, but as long as they remain employees, they will not likely achieve *time* freedom.

PERSONAL FREEDOM = MONETARY FREEDOM + TIME FREEDOM

Most employees cannot be personally free because the very nature of the employer-employee relationship demands that they sacrifice 40 to 60 hours of their time and energy for the paychecks they receive. With the exception of vacation time and sick leave, most employees could not support their current lifestyles without having to continually and substantially work. If they stopped working ... their income would suddenly stop as well.

In my opinion, with some few exceptions, one must *eventually* stop being an employee to achieve true personal freedom. *(Warning: Please do not run out and quit your job tomorrow based on this statement alone! There are other things you must learn first!)*

The Nature of Monetary Freedom

The term *monetary freedom* means different things to different people. Most people think that you have to be rich in order to be monetarily free. I do believe that being rich or becoming rich can be very helpful in attaining monetary freedom … but one only needs to look at our entertainers, sports stars, lottery winners, and dot-com workers to find that it is not necessarily the case.

There have been numerous stories in magazines and newspapers in recent years that tell how dot-com workers became rich … but ultimately lost most of what they had earned or created.

Or taking a look back to the year 2000; many people who thought they were monetarily free with their fat retirement funds and stock portfolio ultimately had their supposed wealth crushed within two years.

I am reminded of a scene in the 1997 movie "Titanic" … when the Titanic was sinking and everyone onboard was looking for lifeboats. The people who could not find a lifeboat would either jump overboard into the churning, freezing waters below, or they would try to hang onto the ship until the very last minute. But either way, all those people were going down.

Today, both retirees and working people in the United States are struggling to find their financial "lifeboats" or "life-preservers" to keep them afloat … while in the meantime, they continue to tread water with hopes that some large ship like the U.S.S. Greenspan, U.S.S. Bush, or U.S.S. Congress come to rescue them. In a vast ocean of people drowning financially, it can be difficult to save everyone.

Prior to the dot-com craze, "get-rich, get-poor" stories revolved around lottery winners who eventually spent all their winnings or entertainers who earned millions but spent it all. One example that comes to mind is M.C. Hammer (a popular musical star in the late 1980's). He had millions of dollars … but still went bankrupt. He was rich, but obviously did not structure his affairs properly in order to stay monetarily free.

People think that monetary freedom is a one-way trip where one day you get the gold at the end of the rainbow and you never have to look back. But the reality of it is - you can get the pot of gold ... but you can also still lose it. Monetary freedom is making sure that your pot of gold is taken care of and that it continues to provide so that you can enjoy it year after year without the fear that it will one day be gone.

The Truth About Conventional Wisdom

I would like to take a moment to comment on the term "conventional wisdom." A casual look into your favorite dictionary or thesaurus will reveal that the word "conventional" means:

- "conforming"
- "adhering to accepted standards"
- "normal"
- "average"
- "ordinary"

Now take the definitions of "conventional" and place it in front of the word of "wisdom." You would get this:

- "conforming" wisdom
- "adhering to accepted standards" wisdom
- "normal" wisdom
- "average" wisdom
- "ordinary" wisdom

Look at those phrases and think about them for a minute. I did this a few years ago ... and I did not like what I saw. I didn't like being "average" or "ordinary," and it certainly made no sense to me to use "average" wisdom and "ordinary" wisdom as part of my mental toolbox. It was the same tired, old advice everyone else used. And you know what? It didn't get me very far.

People who I saw as successful and wealthy personally did not follow "conventional wisdom." I decided I would no longer follow "conventional wisdom" without first questioning the merit of it in my quest for personal freedom.

I needed new thoughts, new ideas, and new ways of doing things ... and part of that was getting rid of the "conventional wisdom" that permeated my life.

Let me give you a few teasers here of some conventional wisdom about money.

- "Stay out of debt."

- "Credit cards are bad."

- "You have to go to college to be successful."

- "Don't quit your job until you have six months of income saved."

- "Save money for your retirement."

Do any of these make you uncomfortable now that I have pointed them out as "conventional wisdom"? I hope so.

I am going to do something that will irritate some of you reading this: I am **not** going to elaborate on these points right now. However, the good news is, I will elaborate on some of them later in the book.

The point I am trying to make here is how pervasive and insidious conventional wisdom and ideas are. They are blindly accepted without any question or thought. In fact, they are so well accepted that it often makes people quiver when someone tries to challenge them. I expect that the establishment will not like my book very much. But then again, most of the establishment has never experienced or earned personal freedom.

This book is about unconventional ideas and thoughts. But this is because having personal freedom is an unconventional concept ... if not an unconventional reality for most people.

Unconventional Wisdom

For some people, the term *unconventional wisdom* may be a bit of an oxymoron. You know what I mean ... somewhat like "government intelligence," "friendly IRS," "cool summer," "warm winter," "jumbo shrimp," and a "tough egg." Somehow, it just doesn't click ... but it does make you ponder a bit.

This book most definitely discusses a lot of unconventional ideas and incorporates unconventional wisdom. Some of this I learned on my own, some I learned from others that came before me, and many are a blend of the two.

From this point forward, if you want conventional wisdom, I recommend you go down to your local bookstore or log on to the Internet and visit Amazon.com or BN.com. There is no shortage of books with conventional wisdom out there.

You can probably find a hundred books talking about:

- Saving money.

- Being debt-free.

- How to be cheap.

- Getting rid of your credit cards.

- Investing for your retirement.

- Investing in mutual funds.

- Picking the best stocks.

- Writing a better resume.

- Getting a better job.

- Getting a bigger raise.

- Getting along with your boss.

- Managing your time better

- Scheduling your time better

The list goes on and on and on and ... Well, you see what I mean.

None of that conventional stuff is included here. This book is about getting to personal freedom as fast as you can, by using different ideas and doing different things.

Remember:

PERSONAL FREEDOM = MONETARY FREEDOM + TIME FREEDOM

On the surface, you may think that this is a business book about money, investing, and personal finances. No, it is not! Firstly, it is a *self-improvement, lifestyle* book that acknowledges money, business, investing, and personal finance as being essential parts of life.

The challenge in dealing with unconventional ideas and wisdom is that it often challenges your core beliefs and emotions. It requires an open mind and objective critical thinking to see the merit of an idea.

There is a saying I am reminded of. I don't know where it originally came from, and there are many variations of it. But the version I like is this:

"The definition of insanity is people doing the same things and expecting different results."

And regarding making changes in your ideas, core beliefs, and consequently your life, I say this:

"If you are afraid of getting a bloody nose, then you should get out of the ring!"

If you cannot understand this, I suggest you get a refund for this book or give it to someone else because the rest of this book won't be able to help you.

The Intrepid Way

2 | Financial Fundamentals

Financial Statements

       I took accounting courses in college. Within my business life, I prepared accounting reports for the companies I worked for. Throughout my personal life, I borrowed money to buy cars to drive.

       What do all three of these items have in common? It was their emphasis on financial statements.

       While there can be several reports that make up a suite of financial statements, there are primarily two of greater significance: The *Balance Sheet* and the *Income Statement* (sometimes called the *Profit-Loss Statement*).

       In formal accounting, they teach that the Balance Sheet has two primary categories: *Assets* and *Liabilities*. The Income Statement also has two primary categories: *Income* and *Expenses*.

       A Balance Sheet is a snapshot of *assets* and *liabilities* on any given day.

       An Income Statement is a summary report of all income and expenses within a given time span. Although the two reports tell different stories, they are also interrelated to one another.

What I will be discussing in this chapter are not the financial reports, but the individual components (assets, liabilities, income, and expenses) that make up a financial statement.

Assets & Liabilities

Author and speaker, Robert Kiyosaki takes creative liberties in redefining assets and liabilities. Much to the upset of many accountants, Kiyosaki redefines formal accounting terms in a way the average person can understand ... and which can also serve them in creating perpetual wealth.

I have paraphrased his definitions of an asset and liability to the following:

An asset is something that adds money to your bank account.

A liability is something that takes money from your bank account.

These definitions challenge conventional accountant definitions. It drives most conventional bankers and accountants insane when they hear these simplistic definitions because they were schooled and conditioned to think much more formally.

Redefining these terms may not be technically correct, but I will say that they most definitely serve us! It is by my learning these simple distinctions that I have been able to create perpetual wealth ... and as a consequence a level of monetary freedom for myself.

It's important to understand what assets and liabilities are because they then lead to the following insights:

- Assets create income.

- Liabilities create expenses.

The simple acid test of whether something is an *asset* or *liability* is to see what would happen to your bank account if you were to purchase or acquire it. If your bank account grows by owning the item, then it is an asset. But if your bank account diminishes, then it is otherwise considered a liability.

Therefore, as a consequence:

- Assets generate income.

- Liabilities generate expenses.

In order to create perpetual wealth, you must create, acquire and accumulate assets, while also minimizing liabilities. The basic rules are:

If you acquire assets, the income will come!

Similarly, if you acquire liabilities, expenses will come!

Here are a couple of things to think about:

If you were to own and live in a mortgage-free house full of equity, for the purposes of building perpetual wealth, it would still be considered as a liability. Why? Because you would still have to pay the expenses of property taxes, insurance, fees, utilities, and maintenance.

The more sophisticated person could then reply, "What if I pulled money out of the equity I have in the house?"

And my answer would be, "You have the money to use and spend, but who and how will you pay that home equity loan back?"

As I write this, the refinancing craze in the United States is still going strong. Because of attractive mortgage rates, people are tapping into the equity of their homes to use as spending money. What they fail to realize (or choose to ignore!) is that the money has to be paid back at some point in the future.

What I have repeatedly seen is that people pull out money to spend, but do not have the ability, knowledge, or the foresight to pay it back!

Thus, a mortgage-free house will still ultimately consume your money ... not add to it. And it will not matter how much equity you have. If you don't believe that owning a home will cost you money rather than earn it, then try buying a much larger home. It may have a lot more equity, but I am quite certain your checking account will notice the difference!

Let me be clear here. **I am not saying that you should not buy a house to live in!** The fact is we all need a place to live. However, you should realize the impact it has on your plan to create perpetual wealth.

Likewise, if you drove a loan-free automobile, for the purposes of building perpetual wealth, it too would be considered as a liability. You see ... you would still have to pay the expenses of tag fees, insurance, fuel, maintenance ... and unfortunately even the occasional speeding or parking ticket.

Again, let me be clear here. **I am not saying that you should not buy a car to drive!** After all, most of us need transportation in order to get to where we need to go. Yet once again you should realize the impact it has on your plan to create perpetual wealth.

The Money Layers

I decided years ago that I wanted to embark on creating perpetual wealth for myself. I wanted personal freedom to spend time on projects and activities I enjoyed.

Building perpetual wealth required me to view money in a completely different way. In the past, the formula was always: work hard, get paid, spend it, and save what was leftover (if any).

After over ten years of working, I found that tired formula to be too slow and ineffective. Quite frankly, it didn't get me very far. I only had check stubs to show for.

The problem with this old formula was that it never really got me ahead of the game ... except for maybe a slightly fatter savings and retirement account. It didn't seem to matter if I made a six-figure salary (which was definitely well within my reach if had I chosen that path).

However, I realized that if I ever stopped working, I would not have enough money to cover all my living expenses. I would ultimately drain my savings and retirement accounts.

Unfortunately, many people have learned this the hard way. The stability of their entire livelihood and lifestyle hangs in the balance of trying to win the goodwill of an employer.

The painful cycle I was living and working under was: work at a job, earn a paycheck, pay your bills, then save what was leftover.

Needless to say, it was very important to break this cycle. Having to constantly work consumed the majority of my personal time and energy. As I said in the beginning chapter, it is nearly impossible to achieve personal freedom without achieving some degree of monetary freedom.

I started to view working for money as being a perpetual cycle ... a vicious circle that had to be broken.

Instead of seeing a circle (as cycles tend to be), I began to look at money and perpetual wealth as *money layers*, to be built and stacked upon each other. The *money layer concept* occurred to me because I viewed myself as embarking on this project to build a foundation: a strong financial foundation to reach personal freedom. It was an insight I had to come to grips with because I realized that creating wealth was not going to be an overnight event. I would not likely come into sudden riches ... such as winning the lottery or inheriting some large estate from a long-lost relative.

I viewed my task for the next few years as a careful and continuous building process. I had expected that it would take me five years, but as it turned out, it only took three years to create enough perpetual wealth to support my lifestyle.

As with all foundations in our most enduring buildings, it begins with the very first layer. Each subsequent layer is then stacked upon one another ... one at a time – gradually – as time goes on.

Using the money layer concept gave me a map on which to chart my financial journey.

There are essentially two types of money layers. There are *income layers* and *expense layers.*

What I was taught in college about accounting was too abstract and impractical for me in the realm of my personal finance. I needed a way visualize the impact of assets, liabilities, income, and expenses. The concept of money layers allows me to singularly and easily view the combined effects of our financial statements: the *Balance Sheet* and *Income Statement.*

If you recall from earlier, assets produce income and liabilities produce expenses.

- Assets >> Income

- Liabilities >> Expenses

Each of these layers illustrates an asset producing a resulting income layer.

- Rental Houses >> Rental Income

- Books >> Royalties

- Online Stores >> Commissions & Sales

- Investment Properties >> Management Fees

- Internet Businesses >> Management Fees

Each of these layers illustrates a liability producing a resulting expense layer.

- Car Loan >> Car payments

- House Loan >> Mortgage payments

- School Loan >> School loan payments

Expense Layers

    Let me first start with the *Expense Layer Chart* because everyone has ongoing expenses.

    In the previous section, I explained that liabilities produce expenses.

Liabilities >> Expenses

    And that it could be shown as an expense layer.

    Using the example of a Car Loan as a liability, our corresponding expense is a Car Payment.

Car Loan >> Car Payment

    Using the example of a House Loan as a liability, our corresponding expense is a Mortgage Payment.

House Loan >> Mortgage Payment

    However, let's say you don't buy a car or house, and instead lease a car and rent an apartment. Do you have any liabilities? No ... not in a technical sense. Because the nature of a lease and rental is that you do not incur a fixed debt. However, it is an ongoing and recurring expense. I refer to it as a *streaming expense*.

    You may not have debt on a car or a house, but monthly streaming expenses are very real. If you do not believe this, then stop paying the rent on your apartment or the lease on your car. Would you be able to continue living in the apartment and drive the car? Not likely. You would be evicted from your apartment and have your car repossessed.

    In these cases, where you technically have no liability, you would view a streaming expense as an expense layer on paper.

- Car Lease Payment

- Apartment Rent

Other living-related streaming expenses that can be viewed as expense layers are:

- Groceries

- Utilities

- Income Taxes

- Insurance

- Entertainment

- Household

When you track and mentally assemble all your liabilities and recurring expenses into expense layers and stack them, you will probably see a money layer chart similar to this:

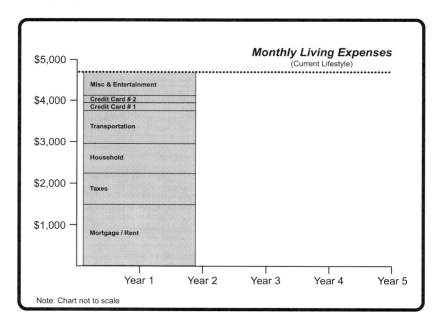

*Please note that I have simplified the labeling by removing the liability name and only listing the expense layer name.

As you can see, each stacked expense layer gives you an idea of how much streaming expenses play a part to your overall monthly expenses. In this sample chart, we see that the expense layers stack up to $4,800 per month.

Within any three month period, you can probably create an estimated expense layer chart that will show you how much your current lifestyle costs you.

For shorter time periods, the above chart works well in giving you an approximation of the monthly expenses you need to track. Over longer periods of time, such as one year or more, the chart is not quite as simple.

For example, over the course of a five-year period, the expense layer chart may look like this:

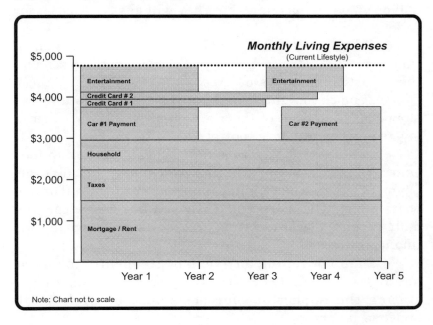

As you can see over the course of time, expense layers can change as you add, reduce, or eliminate liabilities and expenses.

For example, Credit Card #1 is paid off around Year 3, but you still have Credit Card #2 in the 4th year ... but it too is paid off. The car payment is paid off.

There was an entertainment cutback for a year, then it picked up once again.

The gaps you see between the layers are the times when you don't have that particular expense layer in your life. By virtue of not having an expense layer filled, you actually have some financial breathing space. The money that would normally be used to fulfill an expense layer then becomes your extra money.

There are also streaming expenses that are lifetime expense layers for most people. These expense layers would include mortgage or rent payments, taxes, and other household expenses. They exist because they are all a part of our necessities in modern life. They may fluctuate up and down once in a while, but they will always exist ... for as long as you live.

When you step back and look over a particular span of time, you will notice *temporary* expense layers. I refer to these particular layers as *expense blocks*. Some of those expense blocks might include credit card debts and car payments ... and all of them are often temporary expense layers in which we have control over.

Assuming the average new car gets paid off in four years, it is up to you whether you incur the next car payment expense block immediately after the payoff or five years after. The more frequently you buy a new car, the more expense blocks (relating to cars) you will have in your financial lifetime.

I am not telling anyone how frequently to buy or not buy a car. That is entirely up to you. I am simply stating the impact of your decisions as it relates to expense layers.

For most people, there will always be a housing payment, taxes, and ongoing household expenses. Liabilities will periodically be incurred, such as when an old car no longer works and you need to buy another one. In such an instance, the expense layer then gets picked up later.

Expense Blocks

There are also unexpected expense blocks that suddenly appear in life. This could be because of unexpected house repairs or medical emergencies. But whatever the reason, credit cards often absorb those expenses ... which can in turn translate into long-term expense layers.

Unfortunately, what should be expense blocks often become permanent expense layers for many people. These expense layers never seem to go away ... they are ongoing. Circumstances and emergencies keep coming up to keep the credit cards filled, and as such, they remain as expense layers year after year.

A popular way of eliminating expenses is to take out a home equity loan. How would that translate into the expense layer model?

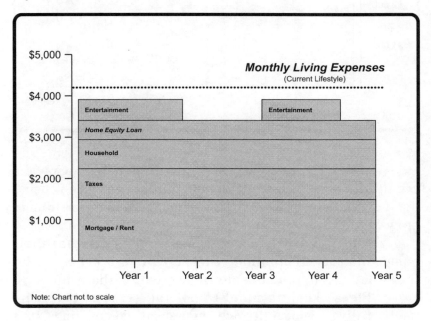

What has happened is that you have rolled what were once temporary expense blocks into one large lifetime expense layer. And to make matters worse, the credit cards that were once cleared now become used again within a few years ... or even less! Furthermore, you have the additional home equity loan, which was for the old debt ... and now you have those credit cards to deal with the newly incurred debt. Yet once again we see that vicious cycle renewing itself. In reality, you would be no further ahead!

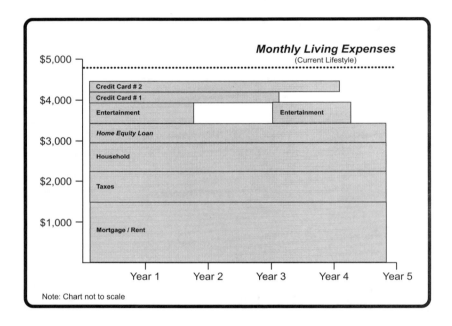

What happens is that new expense blocks are eventually born to replace the old ones. The cycle repeats itself over and over again ... and the layers just continue to grow higher and higher.

This is what happens when people refinance their homes in order to eliminate their credit card debts ... and then they don't stop abusing their credit cards.

Please keep in mind to not take expense layering too literally ... especially over longer periods of time. It is only meant as a visual tool to allow you to view the flow of money differently.

Think About It

Some ideas to think about:

■   Buying short-term liabilities such as cars are expense blocks in our financial lives. They are short-term expense layers. People who consistently replace their cars shortly after payoffs will, in effect, have long-term or even lifetime expense layers. Would you rather have your car expenses become short-term expense blocks ... or do you want a lifetime car expense layer?

■   Buying long-term liabilities such as a house is generally a permanent expense layer. Would you rather buy an extravagant house with a larger expense layer ...or a modest house with a smaller expense layer?

■   There are also expenses that are not liabilities – and they will always exist in our lives. For example, if you do not buy a house, you will likely have to pay rent. One way or another you will have an expense layer for housing. Other expenses that are permanent expense layers include household maintenance, groceries, and utilities. As long as you live, you need to eat, consume utilities, and use other household items. Can you accept that there will not ever be a time in your adult life where there will never be NO expenses?

■   Unexpected financial emergencies that become absorbed into credit cards initially start off as expense blocks. Can you manage to keep them as temporary expense blocks, or will you move them into a permanent expense layer?

■   Expense layers and expense blocks will always exist in our lives. How will you structure the expense layers and blocks in your life?

Income Blocks & Income Layers

The flipside of expense blocks are income blocks. Income blocks are much easier to illustrate and discuss because for most there are usually only one or two income blocks within a household.

Those income blocks look like this:

Wife Labor >> Wife Salary

Husband Labor >> Husband Salary

However, while this may be correct in showing how the income layer is produced, no banker or accountant would ever list "Wife Labor" or "Husband Labor" as an asset ... even though that's what is required to produce the salaries.

They are simply listed as salaries.

So, in viewing the salaries as income layers, we have the following chart - which represents both the husband and wife working:

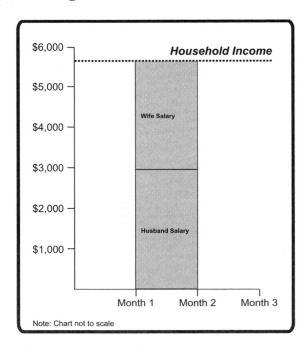

I mentioned earlier that expense layers come from one of two places: you acquire liabilities, which in turn create expense layers, or you simply have recurring expenses that exist as a result of living in modern society.

This also holds true for income layers. They too can come from two different sources: there is income that comes from direct personal labor, and there is income that comes from assets held. Generally, income from personal labor is paid in the form of wages or a salary. However ... these are considered *income blocks* - not income layers.

In the case of a dual-income family, primary income is derived through the efforts of two peoples' labor. They may have some small amounts of income through assets, such as their savings or investment accounts, but often they are insignificant because they are so small compared to their salaries.

For most families today, both spouses must work their entire lives because of their need to maintain two sources of active income. They do so either because they don't know any other way ... or they are afraid to try anything new. In either case, they are doomed to a life of labor.

A Labor-Based Society

Unfortunately, most people in our society are primarily taught to focus and emphasize on creating income with labor, and not with assets. In colleges and vocational schools, most of the emphasis is based on being an employee ... to develop skills and learn how to work for someone or some company, and to participate in a one-to-one compensation plan which is based on one unit of work for one unit of pay.

Some common methods of labor-based compensation for employees are hourly wages or the weekly salary. Self-employed workers receive an hourly fee or a project rate.

Our college system teaches students how to write resumes for potential employers ... not to write business plans to start a business. They teach students how to give the best interviews in order to get hired ... not how to make the best presentation to raise money for an investment. They measure a student's success by the grades and diplomas he receives ... not by the field or business experience and accomplishments he has achieved. Everything is focused on becoming a good corporate employee and to become involved in labor.

Almost 50 years ago, as society started to become more technologically advanced, there was much discussion about the possibility of employees having to work less. There was talk of eventually reducing a standard workweek down to thirty hours! Yet, as time has shown, while our standards of living and productivity are higher compared to previous decades, the average workweek is as high as ever ... with people today easily working 40 to 60 hours a week.

Even in today's information and knowledge-based society, many employees are judged by how much time they spend at the office instead of the output they produce. You see, the amount of time spent in the office *still* matters!

Exchanging your time and energy for money is your labor.

People who have some degree of monetary freedom are not always rich, nor are they without debt and expenses like many people believe. People who have monetary freedom have income layers that come from assets or the management of assets ... not labor.

For example, I currently have several income layers from a variety of sources. A broad view of some of my income layers looks somewhat like this:

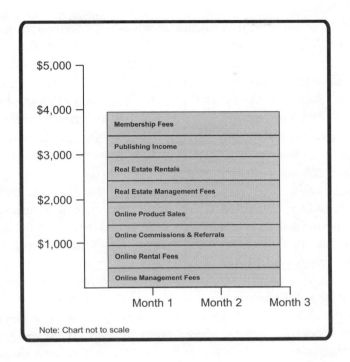

Nowhere in my income layers do you notice salaries or consulting and contracting fees. The reason for that is because I created *streaming income* - or ongoing income that does not require daily labor from me. *Streaming income is money that comes in automatically and "perpetually."* So as such, I refer to the term "perpetual wealth" rather frequently.

I used to earn a good salary in the corporate world as a professional worker and employee. I also earned good consulting and contracting fees as a self-employed expert. But the problem with all of this was that when I stopped working, the income stopped just as quickly.

That is not to say that I do not occasionally receive additional lump-sum incomes from consulting with people or performing one-time or short-term projects. I do those very infrequently on a case-by-case basis as a favor to people I want to work or create relationships with ... not because I depend on them for the majority of my income.

Generally, I use the monies I receive from these projects to produce additional streaming incomes or to reduce any expense layers. Either way, these monies are usually redeployed to improve my money layer positions.

As a matter of clarification, I generally consider income that is created from direct labor (such as being an employee or self-employed expert) to be lump-sum payments or income blocks ... not true streaming income layers.

A test of whether you have an income block or an income layer is to see if you can walk away and not do any work for over 30 days. If your income comes to an abrupt halt, chances are you have a labor-based income block. However, if your income continues, then you have a genuine income layer.

Please understand me here. I am not saying to NOT work for lump-sum payments. It has its purpose. I am simply stating that most people will eventually have to move away from working for only lump-sum payments to work more towards streaming incomes ... to create the income layers needed to reach their own monetary freedom.

I now spend most of my time on creating and acquiring assets ... then subsequently managing those assets. One key to my current personal freedom is that I have a portfolio of assets - some are big, but many are rather small. Every asset generates streaming income, which in turn produces an income layer. Some income layers are bigger than others, but they all contribute to the personal freedom I enjoy today.

The Steps to Monetary Freedom

Years ago, I told a couple of friends about my early successes in creating streaming income. I explained the concept of money layers and the creation of streaming income. At this particular time, I had a breakthrough in having created my first income layer of $200 a month.

I was met with the response, "That's nice. But you can't live on $200 per month." I sarcastically thought to myself, "*Wow! No shit! Thanks for telling me! I couldn't have figured that out on my own!*"

I then tried to explain to them that while it did require initial work to create this streaming income, the money would continue to come in even if I didn't work from that point forward.

This was money that was going to come into my mailbox month after month with very little personal labor. I was actually quite proud of myself because I had never done it before. I knew other people had done it, so I wanted to join the ranks of those who had. I knew it was my first step in creating the perpetual wealth that would ultimately lead me to monetary freedom.

In my mind, that one income layer of $200 meant that I basically had free gasoline, free telephone service, and free utilities for an entire month. I know it was small in the grand scheme of things ... but it was definitely a start! I would not have to substantially work to have those items. More importantly, if I knew how to create one income layer ... I could create *many* of them!

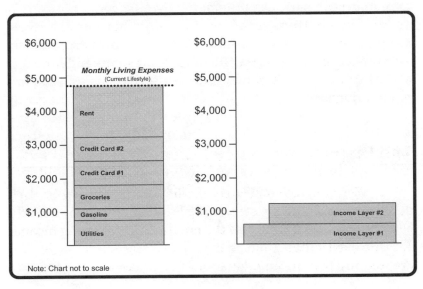

Note: Chart not to scale

However, I realized I did not succeed in convincing my friends about the merits of creating streaming income to have income layers.

They saw it as insignificant and even laughable – to them it was only good for extra spending money. For them, working for the rest of their lives as an employee was a choice they made. And unfortunately for them, from what I now see of their lifestyle and money habits, I have every reason to believe that they will work until a very old age. I see that the pull of an annual salary, of making several thousand dollars a month, even if it is based on their labor, is too strong for them to see the power of a small but streaming $200 income layer.

Fortunately, *I did* ... and ever since, I have not mentioned the idea of streaming income or income layers in front of those friends. I knew they were destined to work until old age ... unless they were willing to change their ideas of money and wealth. With my system of creating income layers, I knew I could achieve personal freedom within five years.

After having created my very first income layer, I then realized that I only needed a few more to have both my car payment and insurance automatically paid for.

Then a few more income layers after that, I wouldn't have to worry about making rent payments. Behold! I saw a light at the top of these steps ... and it was shining so brilliantly and radiantly! The best part of all this was that I no longer believed that I had to be rich in order to be monetarily free. I simply had to focus on building and creating one income layer after another until I exceeded my expense layers. Ultimately, I had a roadmap to my monetary freedom ... and it suddenly became so simple to me. Therefore, I simply focused on this roadmap ... and to this very day ... I am still creating and building income layers. How sweet that revelation was to me!

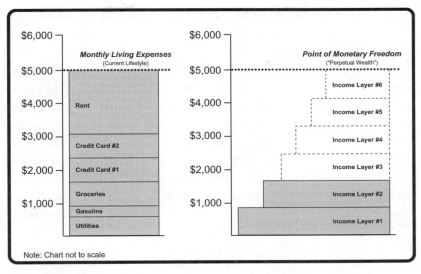

Note: Chart not to scale

As I mentioned, the key to my personal freedom was to continue building income layers to the point where it exceeded my expense layers. When my income layers began exceeding my expense layers, it meant that all of my normal living expenses were covered without me actively working. Again, the above chart is obviously simplistic and not to scale. But it does illustrate how important it is to understand the relationship between expense layers and income layers.

If you look at the chart, you will notice that there is a staircase effect on the income layers. The reason for that is because it generally takes time to create each income layer. Also, the time between the creation of each income layer can vary. There would be times that many months would go by and I was not able to create any streaming income layers, while other times I created half dozen new income layers within a month.

Depending on the opportunity I would encounter, the amounts of the income layers would also greatly vary. Early on, some income layers were very small … from $10 to $20 per month. Why so small? I took those on because they were token payments where my true objective was to establish a new business relationship. Therefore, those tiny income layers were by-products of my creating new opportunities. Other income layers were larger, such as $300+ per month. However small or large the income layer was, I took them in and they took on more significance in my life.

The reason I knew they took on more significance in my life is because I noticed my checking account having more surpluses. I would then use those surpluses to either reduce my expense layers or reinvest to create more income layers. Either way, the successes in creating smaller income layers were rewarded with opportunities to create even more income layers.

With every income layer I created, I was literally one step closer to the top of this staircase to monetary freedom.

Income Layer Supplement

Although I had a roadmap to my own freedom, one of the things that was painfully clear was that there was going to be a period of time (up to five years) where there would be a monetary shortfall. In other words, even if I had managed to create a few income layers, it would still not be sufficient for me to meet my monthly expenses.

That area is illustrated on the chart below. This area represents the monetary shortfall in relation to the expected

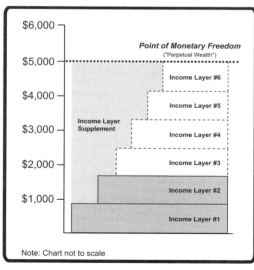

amount of time until I could "escape." In other words - where my income layers equal or exceeded my expense layers.

I refer to this particular area as the *Income Layer Supplement*. It is the "supplemental" income or financial resources that you must have and use to maintain your lifestyle until you become monetarily free.

For most people, the least risky way to deal with this shortfall is to simply maintain your current source of income; which generally means keeping your job and working in your profession and using the lump-sum income earned to create or acquire assets that produce income layers.

If your household has more than one income, it would be far less risky to first get one person out of a job versus having both parties immediately leave to create income layers.

In my situation, I did not have a dual-income. My sole source of income revolved around what I alone could earn.

There is a lot of conventional wisdom that says you should maintain six months of income as reserves. So in other words, if your monthly expenses were $5,000 per month, you would need $30,000 socked away.

Within the money layer model, if I had $30,000 in cash, it would actually last much longer. The reason for that is because IF YOU MAINTAIN your current expense layers, and you continue to accumulate and build income layers, your need to utilize the entire $5,000 per month diminishes with each passing income layer you create.

In fact, most of the consumption will occur during the first half of the journey. It will be needed far less during the last half ... just as you approach the Point of Monetary Freedom. What discourages and scares most people (and justifiably so) is the consumption / spending rate that will occur during the beginning stages ... where there are little or no income layers in existence.

Now, for those of you who want a precise formula in determining how much you need for the Income Supplement Area ... the truth is ... I don't have one. There are just way too many variables that come into play.

But take the most significant factors into consideration. How quickly can you create income layers? How much will each income layer be? Also, will your expense layers fluctuate greatly? These factors can have a significant effect on what the Supplement Income area will be.

For me, I did not have a substantial amount of money saved up. I certainly did not have six months of expense money! I also had both personal and business debts that encumbered the start of my journey. I knew that if I subscribed to the conventional wisdom of saving up for those six to twelve months before I started out, I would probably never get started. After all, most of us know how long it takes to save up for six to twelve months worth of expenses. It can take almost half a lifetime because something seems to *always* come up in life to take a chunk out of our savings. Life is not entirely predictable that way.

Because working for lump-sum income was too time-consuming and took away from my efforts to create streaming income layers, I decided right then and there that I would just go for broke. I had a sufficient amount of credit sources, such as credit lines and credit cards to draw from to start and *partially* fund my journey ... but not for the entirety of it. However, I also realized that my need to draw from those sources would diminish with every opportunity I created ... with every income layer I accumulated.

For the people who knew me before, because I had made a substantial amount of money being self-employed (but also working quite actively), they thought the wiser choice was to continue working while building up my income layers.

For reasons that go beyond the purpose of this chapter, I chose to go "cold turkey" and simply gave up the option of depending on a lump-sum income. For those of you who want to know the rationale of the choice I made, you will find this out in a later chapter.

Please understand that what I did was extremely risky, and could have had tremendous negative

consequences for me financially! I do not recommend for others to do what I did!

I do not want anyone reading this book to think to themselves that just because I did it that way that they should too. That is not my message. My message is for you to have different insights into the money layers ... and especially in creating streaming income in a way that suits your individual needs and timetable.

What I am also trying to illustrate here is that there are many ways to deal with the income supplement issue. As I said, for most people I recommend that someone maintain their job as they build up their streaming income layers, or to team up with their spouse to do so. It may not be the quickest way, but it is definitely the safer path.

In the beginning, when I only had a few income layers, I must admit that it was a painful experience. When I looked at my credit card and bank statements every month, I saw my debt continuing to mount and bank accounts continuing to dwindle. I would constantly pull from other credit sources to fund the monthly income shortfall.

As a side note, it turned out that even though I had given up working regularly for lump-sum income, I did occasionally pick up unexpected opportunities to earn some short-term lump-sum income. Although my *main strategy* was to build income layers, the lump-sum income provided the income supplements I needed to reach my Point of Monetary Freedom. What those income supplements did was give me the extra time I needed in order to reach my goal.

Some friends and acquaintances who saw what I did during that time didn't understand why I never fully committed to any large assignments. In their minds, they often wondered how I could make a living. In my mind, I didn't take the assignments to make a living. I took them either for the opportunities they opened up ... or the extra time they would buy me in attaining my freedom.

Remember: most people think that they have to hoard a bunch of money in order for them to live leisurely. But their plan requires nearly a lifetime to bring to fruition. My blueprint said that all I needed to do was last only a few years to reach the point of escape.

At that point, I could then relax … and decide where I would want to take my life. Because of my own success, it has given me sufficient time to write this book, publish it, and become an author. Additionally, it has also allowed me a greater luxury to work on projects that increase my own wealth, as well as the people I associate myself with.

Becoming Wealthier, Freer, and Happier

When you reach the point where your income layers exceed your expense layers, you then have a decision to make:

1.) You can stop "working" to increase your income layers, just enjoy where you are for the "rest of your life," and start doing what you want to do. In effect, you can "retire".

2.) You can stop "working" briefly to appreciate and enjoy where you are, but then get back into creating more income layers to improve your lifestyle.

3.) You can continue on building income layers without pause.

My recommendation would be to take a pause for at least one or two months to appreciate all that you have accomplished. After all, the original point to creating your income layers was so that you could have more free time to do the things you want … and even relax a bit.

The beauty of taking time off is that you can sit back and reflect on which direction you wish to travel next. For me, it meant taking the time to write this book to document what I had done before moving forward to the next phase of my life. I could continue on doing the same things that got me free because it was the safe road, or I could change directions and create income layers in new areas that I thought might be personally satisfying ... such as writing, speaking, and educating.

Once I was free, I decided that I would embark on improving my lifestyle. There were two fronts involved in improving my lifestyle - one of which was tied into my monetary performance, and another was tied into what I do with my time.

On the monetary front, this meant that **before** I improved my lifestyle, I needed to create the income layer(s) to support it.

For example: let's say I now drive a car that results in a $300 per month expense layer. But, at the same time I am thinking about upgrading to a higher standard of car that results in a $550 per month expense layer.

I would then have one of two choices: I could either make the commitment to buy the upgraded car first and take the $550 per month hit up front ... or I could *first* create new income layers to give me the additional $250 per month.

This last action would allow me to maintain my personal freedom once I take on the $550 expense layer.

I recommend creating the income layer *first* ... before purchasing the upgraded car. The beauty of creating the income layer first is that it teaches you to stay ahead of the expense layer line every time you feel inclined to improve your lifestyle. Also, once you have a performing income layer, it will be yours for many years to come. Furthermore, when the car is paid off three to five years later, you would no longer have the $550 expense layer ... but you would still have the additional income layers you created earlier!

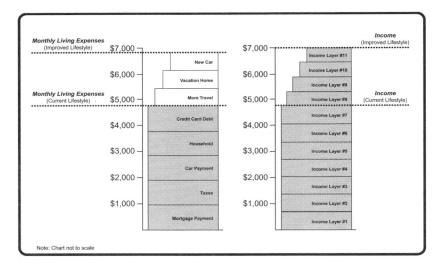

As mentioned, because I have the freedom to choose when to work and not to work, I have the time to take care of my well-being, and to reflect on what future I want to create for myself.

Today, one of the things that is becoming more important to me is to find a potential life partner that can be compatible with my personal and entrepreneurial lifestyle interests. This requires my having the freedom of time to pursue. By having income layers, I can exercise my freedom for a personal endeavor. As the subtitle of this book says, "How to Create the Freedom You Need to Live the Life You Want".

Meanwhile, I choose to continue experiencing more of what life has to offer – and I want to enjoy some of those luxuries. As such, I continue creating income layers that allow me to do this comfortably, while also maintaining my time freedom.

One thing I have chosen to do as I improve my lifestyle is to create a financial cushion (both in terms of cash reserves and income layers). Although my monetary freedom occurred at the time my income layer exceeded my expense layer, I can still be subject to unexpected events that can reduce, temporarily suspend, or eliminate an income layer.

If that occurs, I have a shortfall. But I generally don't worry about it ... because if I don't have the cash reserves I can always pull from credit sources to cover the temporary shortfalls. However, I do prefer having some cash reserves but not necessarily overdoing it. Knowing that cash reserves generally have little leverage, I would much prefer to create additional income layers that are at least 25% over that of my current lifestyle than simply having a stockpile of cash doing nothing.

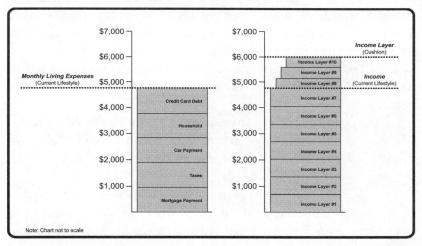

For example, if my expense layers add up to $4,800 per month, it would not be a bad idea for me to continue creating the additional $1,200 income layers to reach $6,000. The extra $1,200 per month can be used for cash reserves, accelerate debt payment, additional investments, or simply as a money layer cushion should I lose ground in other income layers. Short of a catastrophic loss, I will likely have more than enough to cover non-performing income layers.

Creating additional income layers has a two-fold advantage: you can simultaneously create cash reserves with the excess money, while also having extra income layers to off-set any of those that may become reduced, suspended, or eliminated.

Golden Hens

There are primarily two ways of creating income: personal labor, and the creation/management of your accumulated assets.

- Active labor >> Lump-sum income

- Assets >> Streaming Income

When I decided to begin this journey ... when I had no income-producing assets ... I realized that every income layer would be extremely precious to me. I viewed my first income layer as a very important stepping-stone.

Today, each income layer I create requires a small amount of additional management and maintenance responsibility.

Actually, I view myself as a farmer of golden hens. My assets are my golden hens. The income layers that are generated by my assets are my golden eggs, and I am the farmer overseeing this production.

Today, my business is to buy (or breed) more golden hens that I can raise and nurture. In turn, my golden hens lay golden eggs for me. I can always stop watching my golden hens or simply sell a hen to someone else for money ... but then my golden eggs would stop coming.

The friends I spoke of earlier prefer to continually go out and work to kill fresh meat to eat instead of learning how to acquire hens to produce golden eggs for themselves.

In my hen house, I have different types of golden hens: mature golden hens, active golden hens, newly hatched golden hens, and un-hatched golden eggs.

Like a careful farmer, I tend to each type of golden hen. I learn their different personalities and temperaments - but in all cases my goal is to try and get them to become mature golden hens. Some will never become a mature golden hen where it lays eggs easily, effortlessly, and without needing much attention. But it doesn't mean I still don't want them. At the end of the day, if I have a golden hen, I am willing to take care of it and nurture it. You see ... by nurturing even the more challenging hens, they will also lay golden eggs ... while my farming experience and expertise expands.

Good farmers know that it is much easier to take care of golden hens and feast off the golden eggs rather than finding fresh meat to feast off of. Finding fresh meat each and every day to feed yourself is too much work. And if you stop hunting fresh meat to feast on, then you ultimately begin to starve.

My income layers fall into the following categories.

There are some income layers that require relatively little management from me ... such as my real estate. They have been set up and structured in such a way where they require relatively little of my time. Another income layer that requires little management from me is the online rental, commissions, management, and referral fees I receive. My websites do the work by virtue of being on 24 hours a day. These are my mature golden hens. They lay golden eggs reliably and require relatively little attention from me.

I have income layers that are more management intensive ... such as with my online sales business. It requires me to occasionally do some order processing - such as forwarding drop ship instructions and order fulfillments. These golden hens also lay golden eggs. Although they do require a little more of my attention and time, I value them as income layers nonetheless.

Then there are income layers that I am still developing and nurturing. These are newly created or acquired assets ... and they still require my attention. Some will require my attention for only a short time before they mature, while others will require much more patience and nurturing. Yet, some may also simply die off during the nurturing process and never lay any golden eggs at all. It is simply part of being a farmer.

This book is an example of an asset that is being nurtured. If I do my job well as an author and marketer, this book will be valued and become popular - which will then become an income layer for me. If I don't, then I will have to continue nurturing it until it matures into a golden hen or I retire it. If you have bought this book and read this far, then I hope I have done my job by providing value to you while also creating an income layer for myself.

As I go through the developing and nurturing process, I find some hens lay only small golden eggs and will always stay small. Others will lay small eggs now but will eventually lay larger eggs. And then there are those that lay the largest of golden eggs right from the start.

Finally, there are those golden eggs that currently exist only in my mind. These are the golden hens that have not yet hatched. These are the ideas I have, but have not yet made them into reality. But I also value those because one can never tell if an un-hatched egg will one day become a super golden hen that lays super golden eggs.

That is my wish as a farmer of golden hens. To have super golden hens that lay super golden eggs to propel me further and upward in my life.

The Power of Income Layers

Every day someone enters a retail store to buy a snazzy big-screen television, a bank approves a loan for someone to buy a house, or a car dealer approves a new lease on a new car for someone to drive. In these cases, people understand the power of borrowing and credit - where you receive the product today but pay over time.

The power comes from allowing you, as an individual, to buy something that is worth more than what you currently have access to. In essence, you are buying something today with tomorrow's income ... wherever that income may come from. You accomplish this by making smaller monthly payments to a lender.

I wonder how many people actually stop to think about why large companies are so willing to accept small monthly payments from so many people year after year? And yet, why is it that individuals always seem to want ALL their money at once instead of small streaming payments?

The answer is because companies are focused on ongoing business and cash flow by creating huge numbers of streaming income from their customers! These companies understand the power of financing. They will receive more money over a span of time rather than if they tried to get all of the money from you all at once. And there is definitely no shortage of people willing to pay more than the purchase price for the privilege of paying over time!

Once a sale is made, the company continues to make money off of you for many months ... and even years to come. Done on a grander scale, this equates to a massive accumulation of thousands and millions of income layers that will forever sustain the company.

For example, America Online has thirty million subscribers in its network. This equates to nearly thirty million income layers, at $22+ per subscriber. America Online does not try to collect an annual subscriber fee. They are much more content with receiving the small $22 per month from you. They know that more people are willing to pay $22 per month rather than coughing up a lump sum payment of $264 each year. You can do the math to see how much they receive per month ... it's staggering!

My cell phone company charges a monthly fee instead of an annual fee, despite the fact that I have agreed to a one-year contract. My rent is collected on a monthly basis and not a yearly basis, despite the fact that I signed a one-year lease. These one-year commitments allow the companies to create a strong likelihood to receive a predetermined amount of dollars per year from me while they make it financially easier for me by only asking me to pay once a month.

I mentioned that people understand the power of borrowing and credit because it allows them to get something today by using tomorrow's income. The power comes in making it affordable through their monthly payment to the financing company.

It should be noted that one person's expense is another person's income.

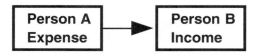

The more expenses you have, the more income you are providing to someone else. That is the essence of how an economy works ... whether it is the local, national, or world economy.

Conversely, to increase your income, you have to encourage others to spend money on your products and services *while providing good value.*

What keeps most employees grinding away are the things they focus on. Most employees can see the value of having expense layers to get what they want today. However, they cannot see the power and value of having *income layers* to get what they want in the near future.

- Using expense layers to get what you want reduces your personal wealth and freedom.

- Using income layers to get what you want increases your personal wealth and freedom.

Instead of looking for ways to create income layers to get what they need to improve their lifestyles, most employees look for ways to create expense layers!

3 | Financial Principles

Income Models

In the early 1990's, I was becoming well established professionally and academically. I had already achieved what I thought was appropriate for the time. I had received my Bachelor's Degree in Business Administration, I had a good position at a good company working for a reasonably good salary, I had earned technical certifications in my field of expertise, and I was getting two nice vacations a year.

I began to think to myself, "What do I do next?"

I thought about starting my own business, but I didn't feel prepared for it … mainly because I never received any training or education in how to *start my own business*. I was only taught how to be an employee in *someone else's business* in college.

Therefore I thought I needed more business-oriented education. What seemed to be the next logical step for me was to get my Master's Degree. So for two years, I worked full time during the day and went to school nearly full time at night to earn my MBA. Because it had taken me seven years to get my Bachelor's degree, I had no intentions of taking a lengthy amount of time to get my Master's.

I then completed the MBA program and earned my graduate degree. While I did think I was better off for the experience ... I really didn't feel any more equipped or qualified to launch my own business than what I did two years earlier!

It then occurred to me the reason why that was! *They didn't teach me the skills of entrepreneurship ... a very special breed of business.* All the education I received was provided by teachers ... who were employees themselves ... and the purpose of the education was to teach us to be even higher-paid *employees*! They did not teach us how to become better entrepreneurs; *they taught us to be better corporate and professional employees.*

It was this realization, in addition to my growing discontent with working as an unappreciated employee that eventually led to my departure from the corporate world later that summer.

Even as I had launched my own business later that year, it took another three years of working as a highly paid self-employed "expert" before I realized that what I was doing and the model I was working under was fundamentally flawed for what I wanted to achieve in my life.

The biggest flaw I was working under was working under a *Limited Income Model*. I realized that my income was entirely labor-based. If I stopped putting my labor in, my income would almost immediately stop.

But I was also limited on how much income I could make because what I got paid was largely based on how much time I put in. It didn't matter whether I got paid by an hourly, weekly, or project rate ... it was all the same. *It was all based on how much production that I alone could generate.* And unfortunately, that limit was often reached very quickly.

That is why achieving a six-figure income for most people is still so highly regarded ... whether you are an employee or self-employed expert. It is relatively a great challenge for most people to get some employer or person to agree to pay you a six-figure salary year after year. You have to demonstrate a very significant value for a company before this would ever occur.

The interesting thing is that if I wanted a six-figure income, I knew what I had to do. I had to work much harder and to work more hours! I had to be willing to sacrifice more of my personal time and energy.

The problem was, based on my calculations, I would still have to work well into my 50's to achieve personal freedom and comfortably maintain the lifestyle I wanted.

And once I got there, how long could I hold on to that six-figure income? Many people in recent years found out the hard way that it is one thing to talk someone into hiring you at a great salary; it is another thing to talk someone into keeping you indefinitely.

Many "fallen angels" have learned this hard lesson after being thrown into the streets by downsizing or bankrupt companies. Regardless, many *still* cling to the old ways. They know of nothing else to do!

During this time, I realized that if I continued with my way of thinking about trying to negotiate better salaries and better contractor rates, I would make a better living … but I wouldn't necessarily live a personally freer and more enjoyable life.

I would be like many other higher-income workers I saw: own nice cars, have a big house, and an even bigger overhead to support. They would continue to grind for 40 to 60 hours a week to maintain that lifestyle until they were 65. And if they ever stopped working for any length of time beyond their predetermined vacations … their livelihoods would come to a speedy end.

Many people have learned the hard way what it means to not have income layers and working exclusively under a limited income model.

In my view, having income layers is a significant step to gaining personal freedom. And if that is all you did, you could lead a very comfortable lifestyle.

However, part of generating streaming income is creating incomes that have few or no income limitations.

The reason so much conventional advice today stresses on saving money is because the advisors' own income is in fact limited and scarce. There is only so much income that one person can generate. There is an artificial cap based on what an employer will agree to pay for one person's services and labor. But can you blame them? After all, there is a limit to how much labor any one person can put in. That is why you may hear people taking on second jobs ... yet at the same time you rarely hear of anyone with a third job. There simply is no more time and energy a person can put in for a third job. Ultimately, their time and their income are limited.

The ability to increase your income and create income layers is largely determined by the underlying system that you are building on.

For example, when I buy investment houses, I do not depend solely on my own ability to qualify for financing. The reason for that is because it is much too limiting. I can only qualify for so many loans before a lender will stop me from purchasing more properties. Lenders are risk-averse. They won't risk that I could lose all the properties and go broke. In reality, what are the chances of every tenant picking up and leaving my investment properties they have called home? From my point of view, it is very slim chance indeed.

As such, I find ways of financing that do not require my own credit and borrowing power. I use owner-financing, as well as financial partners and investor financing. There is no limit to how many owner-financed properties I can take on ... just like there is no limit to the number of financial partners and investors I can potentially work with. Therefore, I do not have a limit to how many investment properties I can buy.

Another example is that I prefer online businesses to physical storefronts. Physical storefronts require too much capital and physical maintenance. While there are certainly physical aspects to every online business, online businesses reach a worldwide market and can be in operation 24 hours a day, 7 days a week. The actual attendance and support on the backend of an online business can be controlled at your discretion. However, the digital storefront that people see on their computer screens can continually accept orders and payments all day and night.

Online businesses are flexible enough for me to sell $500 items as easily as a $5 item. The work involved to sell either is relatively the same. Thus, I can generate far more revenue moving the same amount of merchandise with the same amount of work. Please keep in mind that this is only one simplistic example of thinking and working outside of a limited income model.

I like the publishing business. For example, this book that you have in your hands was written once. However, the potential reward for this book can last a lifetime through book sales and enhanced personal credibility. I can be paid over and over again for a one-time piece of work. Whereas I would never consider being a newspaper writer … the reward for one newspaper article usually results in only one paycheck.

Ironically, so many college graduates have had to write term papers, but they have never managed to put those skills to work for them. In many ways, this book has been easier to write than most term papers because there are not many set rules or formats that must be used within a book. I have some artistic and creative freedom here. And yet, this book has the potential to live on even I after I am deceased. It is all in how you see things and how you apply your skills. I am an author, yet I do not consider myself a writer … much less a very good one. My editor helps make my words sound and flow better.

Likewise, I consider many aspects of websites a form of online publishing. You do it once, but it continues to live on and produce for you.

Prior to writing this book, I produced a few audio programs for business associates. But I never worked for a fee. The problem with working for a fee is that you only get paid once. I would simply produce the programs for free in exchange for the opportunity to sell and promote their products ... but also create goodwill with them for my future projects when I may need their assistance.

The opportunity to sell and create goodwill is unlimited. Simply getting paid for my labor and time is very limited.

At the center of most unlimited income models is your ability to sell. Whether you are selling yourself, your products, services, or credibility, your ability to sell and reach out to the marketplace is paramount. Unlike what they taught in school, salesmanship today is not about cold-calling or being a used car or door-to-door salesman. It is about your ability to communicate, demonstrate, educate, captivate, inspire, and motivate.

The examples I have given you are but a very few ways that I work in an unlimited income model. There is no limit to how many of these types of projects and businesses you can take on because there are always ways to accommodate the growth ... whether it is through hiring others, automation, computerization, investors, or partnering.

Unlimited income models allow you to not only give yourself personal freedom; it allows you to become wealthy ... and even rich! While you have the option to cut expenses, unlimited income models actually work better by *increasing* your expenses. If you increase the *right* expenses, you can actually generate far more income than if you were simply being stingy or frugal.

Limited income models allow you to be comfortable; rarely will it allow you to be rich. In fact, that is why the emphasis on cutting back on expenses is so important. There are simply few options.

The questions I generally ask myself in any project or business I work on are as follows:

1. How much personal time and energy do I have to put in?

2. How much money do I have to invest? How much can I use of other people's money?

3. What is my payoff? Is it financial rewards, credibility, or goodwill?

4. How much of it will I get in return? How often will I get a return? Is it only one time, many times, or infinite?

5. How much do I have to put in to maintain it? Weekly, monthly, annually?

6. How scalable is it? Are there ways to grow it without requiring much of my personal time and energy? Can I outsource it?

If I must use my personal time and energy to work, I generally work on projects that have unlimited income potential with many types of payoffs (financial, credibility, goodwill).

Compensation & Rewards

When I started my journey towards personal freedom, I realized that it was difficult to do everything on my own. I needed to recruit acquaintances and allies to my cause. *Please note that I did not say my family and friends.* (Unless you have very open-minded and supportive family and friends, it has been my experience that you will get very little support from them.)

Many did not understand my need to achieve personal freedom. Most of those "so-called" friends and family thought I was crazy for doing so ... especially when in their eyes I had to take such extreme risks. But the way I saw it, they were not extreme risks ... they were calculated risks. I knew I would inevitably encounter some financial challenges along the way ... and I prepared for them.

It was likewise important to realize that I had to think more openly with greater vision than my employee or self-employed friends. These people believed that other people would only be motivated by money and fixed compensation. Just because *they* won't do anything without an agreement of pre-determined compensation doesn't mean that others won't. That is why they are simply employees. They are trained only to do something for pay. They are not trained to see opportunity. All they can do is provide their labor for compensation.

In the world of entrepreneurship and investing, there are more factors than just money as compensation. Potential for opportunity, goodwill, and credibility are almost just as important.

For example, when dealing with successful entrepreneurs, I know that they *don't* want cash handouts. While they are in the business of making money, they don't want to make money through charity handouts. *They want to earn the business.* So what they want and value are patronage, referrals, and endorsements of their business.

A good way to reward a successful entrepreneur is by providing patronage, referrals, endorsements, and other opportunities for future business. With the exception of my patronage, this financially costs me nothing ... but can win me an incredible amount of goodwill and exchange of services and favors.

When I deal with investors, they also do not want cash handouts. They too want to make money ... but they don't want charity handouts. Investors want good investments and good deals that they can put their money into. They also want good management, credibility, and a track record ... as well as a good return on their investments.

Therefore, when I deal with investors, I don't need to bribe them to work with me. I simply present the fact that there are many investment opportunities with good returns, while also selling myself on management, credibility, and a track record. When I successfully sell myself on my management ability and track record, deal-making becomes much easier.

By using my example, you don't have to pay for investors. Investors will pay you and come to you. You can then attract investors and financial partners to your projects.

With other people, I provide education and information as a form of reward and compensation. These people know that the value of wisdom and experience cannot be easily bought. Even so, if they can in fact buy it ... it is often very expensive. One of the ways I have offered rewards is by freely providing my expertise and insights in the area of computers, networking, and the Internet. While I am no longer in the information technology business, I am still well versed in the usage, language, and mindset of technology ... all of which people, especially my business associates, value.

I have also developed an expertise in real estate investing and financing. As such, I offer that information as a form of reward and compensation. The nice thing about providing education and information is that it costs me very little - but its perceived value is large.

For people who are "up and coming," I offer publicity, recognition, and exposure to those I trust and believe through my online and print publishing ventures. Again, the financial costs to me are very small ... but the perceived value is quite large.

Entrepreneurs sometimes want the opportunity to resell your product, or they may want a piece of the action. If you are starting out and have few financial resources, these are opportunities to expand your business without directly paying out of your wallet.

Goodwill

One of the most valuable rewards I work for is creating *goodwill*. It has often been said that, "it is not what you know, it is who you know." That well-known saying means your personal network of contacts will have a greater influence on your success rather than relying solely on your intelligence, expert knowledge, and hard work.

Having worked in both the accounting and information technology industries, I was often surrounded by people who measured their self-worth by how much they knew. They believed that sheer intelligence and expert knowledge were the keys to success.

What I discovered was that it does lead to a certain degree of success and recognition, but in the end you still have to do the work. You are also limited to how much you can personally accomplish.

Now before I am taken out of context here, I am not saying that developing your intelligence and becoming an expert will not help you succeed in achieving personal freedom. Of course it will! But it is how you use and direct your expertise that will make the fundamental difference.

However, it will be very difficult if you have to be an expert in everything and have to do everything on your own. It simply cannot be done.

Another key to my achieving personal freedom was to enlist the help, sponsorship, and friendship of others.

There are some people who say that people can be bought, while others say they cannot.

I have found that you can purchase personal services and influence people's perception of you with money, but the people whom I most respect and admire and would like on my side cannot be directly bought with money.

They can only be "bought" with *goodwill*.

It is not my intent to be derogatory or manipulative. However, it does illustrate what it takes to win people over.

I figured out very early on that throwing money directly at people was not an effective way to create long-term friendships and relationships. However, what I did realize was that everyone wants to be recognized for what they do and for simply being the person they are.

People want to be acknowledged and appreciated. To truly acknowledge and appreciate someone means I had to show it ... not simply talk about it. I had to be willing to give my personal time and energy.

Because I value my time greatly, I am quite selective to who and how I give my time. I use discretion and judgment to decide whether I want to reach out and be giving of my time and energy.

The act of giving, acknowledging, and appreciating others allows me to create goodwill. *Goodwill* is a general term I use to create positive feelings of affinity, trust, friendship, camaraderie, and kinship. When I create enough goodwill with someone, I generally find that what I get in return transcends any financial or material reward ever imaginable.

Fundamentally, goodwill is not a tangible object. It is an emotion that exists within all people. When you create enough goodwill around the people you deal with, you are rewarded with opportunity, business, referrals, endorsements, and trust.

The power of endorsements, referrals, and trust from the right people can provide you opportunities you had never even thought of. I have had enough successes in my life to understand that goodwill is an instrumental part of creating the opportunities I want in order to achieve personal freedom.

Many of my business associates were initially shocked by my offers to help them with no formal contracts or agreements. When they asked why I would do such a thing, I would reply honestly – in saying that I wanted to create a relationship and goodwill with that person ... and that the way to do that was for me to take money out of the equation to prove myself. I demonstrated my willingness to take a chance on them by allowing them to leave the relationship anytime they wanted. It required me to spend time with them, to be of service to them, and to offer my support to them in their dream projects.

I often decline initial offers for payment for my services ... mainly because payment for my services can sometimes reduce or distract them from the goodwill I am trying to create. Also, I make it clear that I am not in the relationship for a one-time payoff. I tell them that I have faith that things will work out and that they can reward me in a different way sometime in the future.

Some people have criticized me by saying that I am too generous or that I am short-selling myself by not negotiating financial compensation upfront. The problem with that is in the early stages of most business relationships, the financial opportunity is simply too small and too limited in scope. The larger opportunity often comes later, but I have to be patient enough to let it develop and trust in the relationship-building process. To force a predetermined compensation plan would inevitably lead to extinguishing or minimizing the opportunity before it even starts.

My purpose for creating goodwill is to reap the rewards of a long-term friendship or business relationship ... not just a one or two-time payoff.

In looking at the people who have criticized me for "working for free," I have seen that opportunities are not always abundant in their own lives. And while they may be compensated well, few people are going out of their way to assist them in their own endeavors. They have to do it all on their own, and they believe that everything is tit-for-tat. After all, people generally only give after you have given ... and only if you have set that example.

People are so accustomed to negotiating the terms for every business relationship that they end up only getting a one-time payoff. Consequently, because a payoff has already been negotiated, there is very little goodwill created. The pre-negotiated compensation negates the underlying emotion of appreciation and gratitude needed to create goodwill.

Please understand me ... this does not mean that I don't value my time, experience, or services I provide. That is far from the truth. I value it so much that I generally refuse to accept a quick one-time payoff. I insist on keeping our options open to mutually beneficial arrangements.

Nor does it mean that I am doing charity work for people I look to create relationships with. It simply means that in order to make myself extraordinary in their eyes, I have to be willing to do something extraordinary for them. And that in turn has allowed me to set myself apart from others.

In today's world, the concept of "working for free" to create goodwill on a personal level is a very foreign concept for most people ... but nonetheless extraordinarily leaves a great impact. We have been taught that if you do work for someone, you should always be financially compensated for. You see ... that is the essence of the employee mind-set. The fact is that I *do* get paid ... I get paid in ways that cannot easily be seen or measured, but I am often paid many times over. And yes, it eventually results in financial reward.

If you have the initiative to offer to do something of true value for someone unexpectedly, your potential to receive long-term rewards can be tremendous.

The question that inevitably comes up at this point is, "How do you know who to create goodwill with?"

To that, my answer is there is no set way of determining who is "worthy" of your time and who isn't. For me, I generally get an intuition about someone whether they are people of good character and are generally appreciative of life and other people.

I occasionally try to create goodwill with certain people but with unsuccessful results. Either the relationship doesn't work right or they are simply leeches. Overall, the price for my failure and disappointments are small. After all, how much can I lose by doing a good deed or a favor for someone? And yet, the rewards for my successes in generating goodwill and opportunity consistently outstrip the efforts I put in.

Exercise:

- Identify a list of people who you believe could truly benefit from the giving of your talents, services, referrals, and endorsements.

- Out of those people, who do you think would truly appreciate what you did?

- If you were to create goodwill with them, what do you think your long-term rewards would be?

The Lottery Winner's Syndrome

One of the things I often see in people is what I call, "Lottery Winner's Syndrome." These are the people who think that riches equal wealth, that wealth should come instantly and without effort, and once attained, they can spend the rest of their lives doing nothing.

In the United States alone, millions of people spend their labor-earned dollars to buy lottery tickets in the hopes of becoming rich ... *every week*. And while it is true that if you do not play against overwhelming odds, you can never win the lottery, it is also true that your chances of winning big are infinitesimally small. And if you do win the lottery, there are no guarantees that the winner will keep it very long. A lottery winner may get rich quickly, but there are no guarantees that it will translate into long-term or lifetime wealth.

There have been various stories in newspapers and magazines over the years that have followed up on various lottery winners. In many cases, the lottery winners either spent or overspent their money and actually went broke. They were actually worse off long-term than if they had never experienced the winnings. I know that sounds hard to believe ... but it is true all the same.

I hear people saying:

- "When I get rich, I am going to do nothing."

- "If he is so rich, why is he still working?"

- "If he is so wealthy, why doesn't he quit working?"

These people have the mindset that the work they do has to be miserable and unfulfilling ... and that work is to be avoided at all costs. They cannot fathom work as being a form of play, or the need or desire to contribute to society.

For some reason, they believe that once you become rich and wealthy, you should be ready to no longer contribute to society and that you should look towards your deathbed.

The sad reality of it is that these people have never experienced even a small taste of monetary freedom ... much less personal freedom. They may wish for monetary freedom, but they are not really willing to do what it takes to get there. Put quite simply, they are just too damned lazy or ignorant.

We only have to look at the billionaires of the world to learn why they continue to work despite the fact they are wealthy beyond most people's imaginations. Why does Bill Gates, Warren Buffett, or Michael Dell continue to work? They are billionaires. Surely, it cannot be for the money. They are working for purposes that transcend money.

Then the Lottery Winner Syndrome types will also ask:

- "If he is rich, why isn't it he giving it away for free?"

- "Why are they charging for it?"

Often it is the same reason why people will value a $1,000 suit more than a $100 suit. The $1,000 suit may not cost $900 more to make the suit ... even with more expensive material ... but the perception is different.

The essence of economics and business is *creating and establishing value and ultimately receiving compensation for it*. The people who don't understand this are among the people who know very little about business and economics. Businesses don't become or stay successful by giving everything away for free forever. That is work for charities.

People who want riches quickly will have to be dependent on one of the following:

- Marry into a rich family.

- Inherit the money.

- Win the lottery.

- Cash in on insurance money.

They will either have to leech their way into wealth or luck into it ... but most certainly not through building or creating it.

Sam Walton's Theory on Creating Wealth

Wal-Mart is the largest discount retailer in the world today ... thanks to the entrepreneurial efforts of the late Sam Walton.

Sam Walton confounded many of his competitors during the early years ... and even moreso as he guided Wal-Mart's growth. Part of the frustration his competitors had was that he did things that seemed to make little common sense - but worked out to be a tremendous success in the real world. He had insights others did not see.

One of the things he discovered was that the more efficient he was at providing value and discounts to the consumers, the more Wal-Mart was rewarded with business. The reason for this was that he did not underestimate the intelligence of his customers. He knew that his customers would recognize good value when they saw it, and they would reward that by giving him their business.

Another thing Sam learned was that small towns had a lot of hidden wealth ... and that wealth could support a Wal-Mart store. Before Wal-Mart came to small towns, many of the stores available to the townsfolk were simply sleepy little shops run by private individuals. And while there was a great deal of service, people still wanted value and excitement.

Many of the more-established retailers believed that small towns had little wealth to support a major store. But that was why a town was small! What Sam realized was that even people in small towns wanted value and excitement in their products and jobs in their stores.

So when a Wal-Mart came into town and established themselves; offering hundreds of different products at great value all under one roof ... it became a shopper's paradise. It wasn't just the buying; it was the entire Wal-Mart experience. All of a sudden, the wealth that supposedly didn't exist came into being because people now had a reason to spend money and buy things. That in turn led to more hiring. In the past, people simply bought what they needed. But now, people could buy what they needed, as well as things they never even knew they wanted.

The ideas Sam Walton postulated and successfully confirmed would forever revolutionize the retailing world ... it transformed Sam and his family into billionaires, and Wal-Mart was turned into the retailing powerhouse it is today.

The point of my telling Sam Walton's story is that he was an entrepreneur. He thought differently because he saw things differently ... and then he carried those ideas out.

Now, I am not so bold to compare myself to the genius of Sam Walton. However, what I am saying is that I was willing to borrow a couple of the ideas that made Wal-Mart so successful and incorporated them into my own entrepreneurial and investment ventures. For those of you who want to learn more lessons from Sam Walton, I recommend you find the book he wrote, "Sam Walton: Made in America." It is a great read with some wonderful business and life lessons.

The idea of creating wealth in a smaller town is not only possible, but also it can actually be much easier there.

For me, this meant the barriers of entry to create and buy investment properties were lower. I would become a bigger fish in a smaller pond.

When I announced years ago that I would leave the great city of Atlanta to go to the smaller city of Columbus, Georgia, nearly everyone questioned and ridiculed me as to why I would do a thing like that. They thought it was foolish and that smaller cities and towns had few opportunities. Although in my mind ... I saw plenty! I may travel and visit many larger cities, but I can no longer see the day that I would ever move back into a larger city to permanently live. I love the lifestyle of a smaller city, but I find plenty of abundance as well.

The limited financial resources I had would be magnified in small towns. After all, it is far easier to buy a 3-bedroom house in Columbus, Georgia than what it would be in San Francisco.

I also had fewer competitors. I could bring the innovative ideas that would come from larger, more cosmopolitan cities into a smaller, less sophisticated town ... where the value of what I had to offer would be more impactful.

Today, I believe part of my success has been my willingness to take what I learned in the bigger cities and then moved into a smaller one to implement it all.

Big People do Big Things

I have heard people say that people who want to be rich and wealthy are greedy people with large egos. While this may be true in some cases, I don't think that there are any shortages of poor or middle-class people with large egos.

The question behind this is, "Why accomplish something beyond your own survival?" These people cannot understand that "making a living" isn't all that difficult. Nearly anyone can get a job to make a living and get by ... it takes something more *within* to achieve more *outwardly*.

I also hear from people that they would be satisfied if they could make enough money or have enough wealth to simply support themselves. The problem I see with that kind of thinking is that those are the same people who don't provide much to society. They are not the great movers and shakers of our world.

I will admit from personal experience that it does take a larger than normal ego to really want to grow big. But on the other hand, that part of the ego both serves and hinders me.

My ego serves me in that it allows me to reach further and beyond what I might normally do to simply be comfortable. Yet, it hurts me in that sometimes it makes me a bit arrogant and self-righteous ... or that I think I know more than I truly do.

As a whole I do acknowledge that *ego* allows me and others to achieve goals greater than ourselves. But there are also many people whom we respect in the business world that have even larger egos.

I have not yet met any of the following individuals on a personal level to give a first-hand account of what kind of people they are. However, I will leave it up to you if these people had big egos. And in doing so, did the world benefit for having what they created?

Can you possibly imagine:

■ Walt Disney World without Walt Disney?

- Wal-Mart without Sam Walton?

- Microsoft without Bill Gates?

- Dell Computers without Michael Dell?

- Star Wars without George Lucas?

- Rocky Balboa without Sylvester Stallone?

- Star Trek without Gene Roddenberry?

- E.T. without Steven Spielberg?

- Rock and Roll without Elvis Presley?

The list is virtually endless.

For me, regardless of whom those people are or what they were truly like, the world has benefited greatly because of the "bigness" of these people. They achieved great and grand things.

All of these great achievements could not have happened without these founders and creators having big dreams ... and yes ... big enough egos to believe they could achieve such things.

Please understand that I am not making it wrong for people who prefer to live a more humble and conservative lifestyle. However, the truth of the matter is that the scope of influence for most average people is fairly small and limited. Even if they want to make a bigger contribution to the world and serve more people, they are unable to do so ... not because of their skills or abilities - but because of the mental limitations they have imposed on themselves in their minds and lifestyle.

It does not upset me that people would prefer to live a smaller scope of lifestyle where they simply provide for their family. We should be so lucky to have even more people. There are so many deadbeats in the world.

What upsets me is when those people automatically pass judgment on others who strive to be greater than themselves ... simply to justify their own smallness and limited scope.

The fact is when you stay small; you can only help so many people in society. When you become larger, your scope of influence is greater and you can potentially affect more change. My goal is to help make more positive changes in the world. Part of that strategy was for me to take the time to write this book, and then personally publish it to get it out into the world at large.

I would even venture to say that many people who choose to stay small and only worry about making enough for themselves are sometimes more selfish than the wealthy people who provide opportunities to others, pay more taxes, give to charities, and change the communities and lifestyles of others. Wealthy people take on a greater sense of responsibility.

So which do you want to be? Would you prefer to simply make enough so you can support yourself? Or would you like a shot to step up to a larger scope and make a difference on a grander scale? It is up to you.

The Truth About Credit Cards

Credit cards seem to get a bad rap in the public media. You constantly see books and so-called experts publicly bashing credit cards: how bad they are, how dangerous they are, and so on.

True ... there *are* credit cards that have the fine print where they hide high interest rates loaded with hidden fees and annual costs. However, there are also many cards that do not have any of this.

The so-called "experts" blame the credit card companies for offering their cards to potential customers to abuse. They claim high-risk people are "not qualified" to have credit cards so they shouldn't get them. That may be so, but it is not the "experts" that are taking the financial risk to offer the cards to new customers. The credit companies are.

Last time I checked, I didn't see any of those experts offering anything but their criticism.

This is like saying that chocolate companies should stop selling their candy bars where overweight people shop because they are at a high risk of buying more chocolate in order to become even more overweight! Recently, there was a court case where someone tried to sue McDonald's ... claiming that it was their fault that he was obese. Apparently, he went to McDonald's everyday to eat and he became obese over several years of eating there.

I thought to myself, "What idiot doesn't know that McDonald's serves fast food that is fattening? And did McDonalds hold a gun to this guy and say 'Buy our food or else!'? Were there no other restaurants to eat at?

I think not.

In any case, I digress. This type of attitude takes the responsibility off of the person truly responsible: the consumer - or more appropriately - the spender.

There is nothing inherently wrong or evil about credit cards. The credit card is a financial tool used to convey payments in a manner much like checks, money orders, cashiers checks, and debit cards.

It is true that there are many financially irresponsible people, and perhaps they are truly unable to control their buying habits. However, the fault lays with the user of the credit card ... not the credit card companies.

There needs to be more of an emphasis on educating people on how to better use their credit cards, control their spending habits, as well as in dealing with the underlying emotions and motivations of buying and spending.

I have been an active user of credit cards since I was nineteen. I love my credit cards! Even though I have been a user of credit cards for most of my life, I don't generally carry a balance. The times I carried credit balances have been times when I needed it - such as when unexpected expenses came up and they needed to be taken cared of. Credit cards have always been a helpful financial instrument for me. But then again, I had at a young age realized that financial power comes with financial responsibility.

I have often used credit cards to fund entrepreneurial ventures that no bank would even bother to look at much less approve a loan for. Sure ... I admit that I have lost money on those ventures, but I have also made money with them.

Often, I would simply use my credit cards to buy office supplies, computer equipment, software, educational materials, business travel, seminars ... things to that effect.

What people fail to realize is that there are times when it's better to pay interest now rather than to let time pass. For example, a seminar taken this year is often more valuable to me than one taken next year. Is the interest I pay for that one year worth having the information one year sooner? Often, if it is unavoidable, I will commit earlier.

No one would ever argue against the idea that it's better to learn how to add and subtract numbers while you are in elementary school rather than in high school. The reason being has to do with the cost of staying ignorant for a short time versus a long time. There often is a negative ripple effect for delayed knowledge.

As an entrepreneur, I respect credit cards and value them greatly. People are running around saying that using credit cards is bad, and that all interest you pay on credit cards is likewise bad. This is because most people buy consumer "junk" that has little value thirty days after it leaves the store.

I don't make these kinds of generalizations regarding my finances. I make finer, more personal distinctions for myself. If I go out and eat at an expensive restaurant and charge it to my credit card, I know I have very little to show for it when the monthly statement comes in. However, if I buy a new color printer for my computer system, there is a good chance it will continue to provide ongoing value. It isn't the credit card; it is what you use it for.

I know what is required and what the costs are for charging on credit cards, as well as all the possible consequences. I have learned to be a responsible and knowledgeable user.

People who know me will agree that I am fairly generous with myself when it comes to self-improvement or business-related expenses. The reason I am so generous is because more often than not, I don't buy impulsively. I evaluate the money I am going to spend versus what I can get out of it. To me, it is an investment. And if it is something that I have determined as mandatory, I then see if the interest I have to pay is worth getting it today versus waiting until I have all the money. It is all a matter of return on my investment.

Instead of teaching people how to think about and evaluate what they buy, many people simply say that credit cards are bad. I think that is an overly simplistic judgment and a very limiting point of view ... especially when it can be a great source of entrepreneurial money.

The fact of the matter is the major companies use debt to finance their growth and success; they know it is a form of leverage. If they borrow money at 10%, they know it is their job to generate 20% or more.

Don't get me wrong. I do believe that there is a point of having too much debt. This is called *overleveraging*.

If you eat too much ice cream, you can become obese. But does that automatically make eating ice cream bad? No! The fault lies with the person who is doing the eating.

There is this never-ending cycle that I see some people go through: people have poor spending habits. They spend poorly, regret it, and spend months or years paying off a debt that gives them very little benefit. Instead of taking on the responsibility themselves, they put the entire blame on the credit card company.

As I said, I have not carried credit card balances for most of my life. And the times in which I have carried credit balances, it has mostly been for business-related expenses or unexpected personal expenses.

As an entrepreneur and investor, financing is crucial. And unless you have become well established, financing can be quite the challenge. So, if I cannot formally obtain financing from banks or investors, then I am required to finance it myself.

When I left the corporate world, I had only a little bit of money saved up. But I did not let that stop me from leaving ... partially because I understood the power of financing and credit cards. I didn't have all the equipment and credentials I needed to become a successful freelance technology instructor. Some of the things I needed included a notebook computer, additional desktop computers, software, supplies, as well as attending seminars and conventions.

I felt quite confident that I would be successful, but I would be required to ramp up. Ultimately, I was faced with the "chicken or the egg syndrome." I didn't have all the required money to ramp up and be successful. And without being ramped up, I couldn't make the money to pay all the startup costs.

Because leaving the corporate world required some contrarian's thinking on my part, I surmised that I would have to find a way to make things happen to get ramped up. As it turned out, I managed to barter my services by offering my time to perform pro bono work. However, I also didn't hesitate to spend, get into debt, and pay the interest ... because the spending I made would ultimately make me money. Yet, I was getting into debt by investing in my business and myself ... not junk that sat in the closet.

As a result of my decisions, I became fully ramped up within a year. And when I did, it was only a matter of months before I paid off the underlying debt. *I did most of this with credit cards.*

Now, most people will say that this was risky. What if I didn't make it? I admit that there is always the possibility of failure, but the bottom line is people who don't make the leap lose anyway. They are trapped in a job with limited income and limited time. They then spend money by charging their purchases to their credit cards. In turn, these purchases don't make them any money, and they ultimately spend most of their lives repeating this vicious cycle.

Diminishing Effect of Reducing Expenses

At this point, you should realize (as I had years ago) that the road to personal freedom is very possible. You *do not* need to be rich to create perpetual wealth and live a life of personal freedom.

There are fundamentally two ways of creating perpetual wealth:

- Increase income layers.

- Increase income layers while reducing expense layers.

We seem to live in a culture of great extremes in the United States. We see a life of extravagance and excess on our televisions and movie screens on one end ... while on the other end we see a world of scarcity and desperation on the streets of our slums and ghettos.

In the realms of the middle-class, there are people who believe they need to work harder and demand more raises to better their lifestyles. Then there are also those people who believe they should start cutting coupons and bottom-feed (acquire things very cheap or free).

I am a first-generation Chinese-American. As such, I have plenty of exposure to Asian cultures ... which place a strong emphasis on frugality. People who come from Asian cultures tend to first look at cutting back on their expenses ... with some to an extreme amount.

Subconsciously, the thought is that money is scarce ... so the first thought is to simply cut back. I have no problems with people cutting back expenses; except for those people who do it to extremes.

I do believe that there is a point of diminishing effect in the continual emphasis on cutting expenses. The situation is not helped when so much financial advice today revolves around the mentality of clipping coupons or buying at the flea market. However, people who live in extravagance they can't afford could learn and adopt a few good habits from frugal people.

For most people, I do believe that there is room for paring down expense layers. In today's society, we have so many things taken for granted as necessities in our lives. It could be the weekend dinners, the annual vacation, the third telephone line, the second computer, the second television, the third VCR, the third cell phone, the third car for the teenage child, the Christmas gifts, the magazine subscriptions, and so on.

These are often absorbed into our credit cards ... when actually they should only be short-term expense blocks. But unfortunately many people convert those short-term expense blocks into long-term expense layers - such as when they use a home equity loan (long-term expense layers) to payoff (replace) their credit card debts (short-term expense blocks).

It is not my place to tell people what their standard of living should be; it is a very personal choice. However, there generally is a financial price to pay for choosing a higher standard of living versus a lower standard of living in the early stages of creating wealth. This price can be seen by how high your expense layers are as compared to how much progress you have to make in creating the offsetting income layers.

For some people, I believe that this would be a monumental task. It can be done, but it would require more time and effort to create income layers to match the higher levels of the expense layers.

Conversely, I also realize that there are negative consequences by living too low a living standard from the extreme cutting back of costs. There are consequences that go beyond the simplistic expense layer model I have described and shown you in this book.

For example, not having a car in New York City is fundamentally different than not having a car in Atlanta. Not having a car in New York City will probably save you money, minimize expenses ... and not to mention the aggravation of parking. You can eliminate that expense layer easily in New York City. However, you will still have a transportation expense layer because of bus, subway, and taxi fares.

Yet, while not having a car in Atlanta may help minimize expenses, you would also eliminate your source of income by not being able to get to work in a timely manner. Anyone who has been in Atlanta realizes that having a car is almost a necessity of life there.

There are some considerations that we must make for ourselves and the area in which we live.

How about people who try to save money by not using the air-conditioner in the summer heat of the South or the heating furnace in the deep winter cold in the North? Every year there are news reports of people who have died in the summer heat or the deep winter cold. I think that most of us will agree that saving in these areas is not the way to go ... especially when it can potentially be life threatening.

Here is another example:

A family of four living in San Francisco will probably have a difficult time trimming expenses if their expense levels are already at $4,000 per month. It is very difficult to minimize expenses when you are already at rock-bottom expense levels for the area you live in.

I see too many supposed "financial experts" giving generalized advice without making distinctions for different circumstances and environments.

Because people blindingly believe so-called "financial experts" when they say that everyone must save money and minimize expenses, they don't realize that they are sometimes beating their heads against a brick wall.

There is a point of diminishing effect in the strategy of only minimizing expenses. At some point, you will have cut back all you can before winding up living in the streets. Sometimes the personal energy required to shave off that last $10 per month is simply not worth it.

When you have hit the point of diminishing returns of minimizing expenses, there is only way to start focusing: the income and leverage side.

Each time I quit cold turkey, plummeting to a zero income, I always knew going in that I would have unavoidable expenses. No matter how much I saved and cut back, I would still have a certain amount of expenses, such as my car, insurance, food, housing, and so forth. I knew that after a certain point in looking at my budget there was only so much money I could save and expenses I could cut. Any more thought and effort in cutting expenses was largely going to be a waste of my time and energy.

There are some people that look day in and day out to reduce expenses that virtually cannot be reduced. They persist in being cheap, clipping coupons, buying at flea markets, and engaging in activities that use $20 worth of their time to save $5. That makes no sense to me at all.

Bottom line: *Once expense levels have been minimized, all efforts should be shifted towards creating and generating income.* Small companies have become great companies by focusing on growing business and revenues. Ordinary people become wealthy by focusing on growing their business and income ... not solely on minimizing expenses and saving money.

For the people who have too many goodies in your house ... and you know who you are! You are the people who have all kinds of sports equipment or memorabilia lying around unused. You are the people who have the unneeded extra cars, boats, big-screen televisions, closets stuffed only with designer clothing, and are members of all the "cool" clubs. You can probably work on reducing expense layers.

You need to start focusing inwards, getting things under control, and STOP worrying about keeping up with the "cool people" or latest fads. Once you do that, you can once again focus outwards ... but this time around you will be looking for opportunities to create income layers instead of getting the latest gizmos and gadgets.

For the people who already are frugal ... likewise you all know who you are. You are the people who only buy generic brands, use candles for light, have little furniture, no food in the refrigerator, and will not read any books that you can't get from the library. You probably don't need to devote any more time in reducing expense layers. You need to start focusing your thinking outwards to create income layers ... instead of inwards on expenses.

It is the best way out to personal freedom. Take my word for it.

Saving Money

The term "save money" brings two different meanings to my mind:

1. Reducing expenses.

2. Accumulating money for future use – both short- and long-term.

We discussed the diminishing effect of reducing expenses in the previous section.

In short-term money saving, you might accumulate money from your disposable income or tax refund, and then use it as a down payment for a new car, house, or investment property. In long-term money saving, you may be accumulating money for retirement.

I am a proponent for short-term savings, where you save up for specific needs. Saving up for a small down payment to buy a new car is probably a good use of money ... especially if your old car is in disrepair or requires excessive maintenance. Saving up a down payment to buy a house where you will live for more than five years is also probably a good idea. Saving up for a down-payment to buy an income-producing investment property is a great idea ... IF you know what to buy.

I am not a big supporter for long-term savings ... especially as a plan for retirement. It is simply just too slow and impractical a practice for most people.

I wonder how many people in their 50's and older are still thinking that they will save up enough money to provide them with twenty years-worth of future living expenses?

I have heard over the years that people should save three to six month's worth of income before you change jobs. This old idea obviously has not been updated for the 21st century. Nowadays, many of the job changes are involuntary, sudden, and without warning.

Also, exactly how long does it take to save just one month's income for reserves? Most people probably use most of their one-month's income just for living expenses. How much could possibly be left? Will it take two, four, or six months to save up one month's worth of reserves? I am willing to bet that taking six months to save a month's income is quite optimistic.

In my own life, I found that it actually takes many months to save just one month of income. The problem with trying to save six months of income is that it requires much more than six months saving it! It could take years to save that much ... if at all! If I were to follow the old, tired advice, I would still be working to save it instead of being personally free to further increase my wealth.

For me, it is a terrible plan and just plain bad advice to give people.

Hoarding Money

The whole premise of saving money year after year is really the act of hoarding money for yourself year after year ... never to be released again until that magical time of retirement or dire emergencies in your life.

Saving money is also based not only on the premise that money is scarce, but also that it must be hoarded year after year so that you can survive in your older years. Furthermore, it is also assumed that in order for you to have money, you must first "own" the money.

I have discovered that money is quite plentiful. The more skilled I am in tapping into money; raising, managing, and investing it, the more money comes to me. It allows me the freedom to enjoy writing, teaching, speaking, and traveling. I get the time to study, learn, and be with abundant and like-minded people, who give me counsel, ideas, and knowledge to be even more effective.

I now create wealth and money for myself because I know how to manage and direct the flow of money, with tangible and intangible resources. In economics, this is called *capital management*.

The reality is that the greatest wealth in the world has never been based on the premise of solely saving money. Wealth has been created by either investing money or spending money to create value.

In any profession or industry, people or companies built their wealth and fortune by investing or spending their money on employees, real estate, equipment, marketing, research, development, and so on.

They made their fortunes by using money and resources to create value for their customers. They were rewarded by the gifts of ongoing patronage, subscriptions, fees, etc. ... which in turn increased their wealth. They then took that wealth and repeated or expanded upon the cycle in order to create larger businesses and investments.

Now, I want to point out that I am not endorsing the idea of spending or investing money recklessly. I am not saying that you shouldn't save money in order to invest in or start a business. I am also not saying that you shouldn't save some money for "rainy days."

What I *am* saying is that using the sole strategy of "saving money" to create wealth and retirement fundamentally goes against the nature of money; which is to be harnessed ... not hoarded.

For most people, saving is too slow and too ineffective a strategy to make any kind of difference in their lives. In my opinion, it is the road to mediocrity and averageness. You might be able to support yourself when you retire, but you will likely have to live a life of frugality based on limited income. You will have provided employment to no one, given little to few charities, and provided little impact to the world around you because you hoarded money.

Freedom Without Riches
➤

Some time ago, I chose to attend different events that literally took me cross-country; from Atlanta, to Phoenix, then Austin, and finally New York City ... all within a three-week time frame. It was an exhausting three weeks of primarily living in hotels. However, I did stop at home in between trips for a day or two to get a change of clothes and rest before having to leave again.

While I was on the road, I simply checked in on the Internet periodically to monitor my business activities and finances.

During the quiet moments of my travel, I realized how fortunate I was to be able to get away for three straight weeks to enjoy the events I attended. I met and socialized with interesting and like-minded people, whereas most other people had to go to work at a job they didn't like and exhausted them.

Conceptually, I knew I had made into reality the fact that I didn't have to be rich to have monetary freedom. Part of that monetary freedom was having the peace of mind in knowing that I could continue to be away while the money would also continue to come in. As long as I continued to effectively manage and nurture my assets, the money will continue to come.

Now there may be some cynics who will say that I still work, and if I stopped working that my money would eventually stop coming in. I admit that this is *partially* correct. But again they probably have Lottery Winners Syndrome where they expect to get something by putting in virtually nothing.

In my personal life, I tend to stay up late at night and I get up late in the morning. When I wake up, I do things I have to do ... but I don't consider a lot of it "work" because I do not dislike what I do. Furthermore, many other things don't require a lot of my time and effort.

In fact, if I wanted to rest on my laurels, I could live a semi-retired and conservative lifestyle "working" only ten hours a week. The more effective, efficient, and experienced I am, the less time and effort I have to put in to create the same or greater results.

No matter how efficient an employee is and no matter how many technical advances in automation or computers, the amount of time an employee puts in will *always* matter. Their productivity will go up, but they still have to work full-time and as such, they will never gain much time freedom. And remember: without time freedom, it is very difficult to achieve personal freedom ... to become wealthy and live the life you want.

I strive at all times to be a better thinker, planner, and manager ... not a better laborer. A better manager and thinker gets more done in less time. A better laborer gets more done in the same amount of time. There is a huge difference there!

**"Income based on assets set you free.
Income based on labor keep you imprisoned."**

The Value of Money is Relative

When I decided to create my own monetary freedom, I had to come to terms with the realization that if I decided to quit my current lifestyle, where I no longer had an income, I would become reliant on the odd jobs, credit lines, and credit cards I had.

Although I knew that there would be many opportunities to create income layers and build up my business, I would also have to take care of my immediate needs; namely continue making rent payments, pay utilities, putting gas in my car, buying groceries, and also have funds to still buy books, courses, attend events, office supplies, and other business-related expenses.

Additionally, I knew that real estate was essential to my strategy; therefore I had to allocate some resources to acquire real estate.

I had to seriously challenge my core beliefs and assumptions. The dilemma was that my personal financing sources were limited. I did not believe that my personal financing sources should be substantial enough to last me five years or more, but I did want it to last as long as possible. I only needed it to last long enough so that I was no longer drawing from it.

I have known about the cost of living since I was eighteen years old. For example, the cost of living in San Francisco or New York City would be much higher than that found in Atlanta ... even though each one are considered to be a major city.

Also, because I wanted to conduct business and buy real estate, I knew that the price and demand for real estate within those areas would be prohibitive ... and would be a significant barrier of entry if I had lived and did business in those places.

With these observations, I realized that although the American dollar was accepted in all fifty states, the weight of money varied greatly from state to state ... even from city to city within a state.

So if I had $20,000 in financing lined up, it could last a year in a smaller town in Alabama or Georgia versus lasting only three months in California.

Furthermore, if I had $5,000 to put towards real estate, it would be considered a great joke in high-appreciating areas of the country ... whereas it would otherwise be considered as a significant down-payment towards an investment house in a small Georgia city or town.

The weight of the American dollar is relative to the area in which you live, invest, and do business. I realized that if I wanted to magnify the power of my funds, I would have to move to an area where $1,000 got me a whole a lot more.

The Tides of Money

One of the things I have learned about wealth are the "tides of money" ... money flows in, and then money flows out - and usually in unequal amounts. This is what I refer to as the *Tides of Money*.

I have noticed many people don't like change ... especially in their financial status. I hear people say that they want a steady job with a steady income. It is more important for most people to have a steady income rather than have a *higher* income.

In economics, we learned that a business cycle consists of recessions and depressions, expansion and prosperity.

Likewise, on a smaller level, entrepreneurs and investors have to be aware and prepare for the tides of money that will inevitably occur.

Since the movement of money is normal and expected, there will be times when money is plentiful and other times when money is tight.

People who believe money should always flow inwards will be ill-prepared for economic downturns and financial setbacks. Also, people who believe that money is always tight will not be prepared for sudden growth and unexpected business opportunities.

In conventional terms, managing the tides of money is called *cash flow management*.

The term "tides of money" is much more appropriate because the term *liquidity* is often used in financial management. Liquidity implies that money *ebbs and flows*.

It is your ability to manage these money tides that determine whether you are to be successful long-term. How well you steer that sailboat through those ebbing and flowing tides will ultimately determine whether your boat will sink or float.

The Intrepid Way

4 | The Work Principles

Are you a Prostitute?

Prostitution is often known as the world's oldest paying profession. Yet, it is not an occupation that most people aspire to. There will inevitably be people who say they choose prostitution as an occupation because they enjoy their line of work. However, I will venture to say that most "only do it for the money." In a broader sense, being a prostitute is doing a job solely for the money.

How many people do you know say that they are working for someone or in a particular job "just for the money"? They get no pleasure, satisfaction, or pride from their work ... only money. *They are prostitutes in life*.

At some point in our lives most of us have been guilty to some degree of being "prostitutes" - where we are "only doing it for the money." By being fully aware of this fact, this will be the first step in making a change.

It is important to know that you can do the same job at different times in your life; you can be an artist first and later become a prostitute. You see ... the difference lies in your motivation in doing a job.

Each time I became discontent and disliked my job or business, I would begin to feel like a prostitute because I was "only doing it for the money." I didn't call myself that consciously, but I knew my heart was no longer in the work or business I did. In turn, I would quickly plan for a way to get out. However, sometimes there were no plans ... I simply just got out.

You may want to pause for a moment here and ask yourself, "Are you doing what you are doing today only for the money?" Be truthful to yourself. You don't even have to say it out loud.

I am guessing that many of you won't like the answer. If you were perfectly happy with what you are doing, then you would never have purchased this book to read.

An Employee's Focus

I mentioned earlier that it is highly unlikely that most employees will attain personal freedom because of the basic premise that:

Personal Freedom = Time Freedom + Monetary Freedom

The reason for this is that even if an employee accomplishes monetary freedom by creating the income layers to support them, they will not have time freedom. If you are giving up 40 to 60 hours of your best time and energy to someone else, you will not likely have enough time left over to do all the things you truly want.

Although at first thought, you may be wondering why someone would continue to work as an employee if they had achieved monetary freedom. Well ... you may be surprised at the responses! Here are a few reasons:

- Some people have worked so long that they say they would not know what to do with their time if they did not work (you tend to hear this from older people).

- Some people will lose their sense of identity and self-worth because it is tied to their profession and position of employment.

- Some people will still not have the emotional courage ... even if their finances are provided for. Their fear of financial loss is so strong that it will keep them as employees.

The biggest reason I hear and see is:

"Employees stay employees because they focus on things that keep them employees."

Personal freedom is a choice. It is a lifestyle choice that requires an emotional leap to claim the ultimate prize.

They think and focus on their steady paychecks, retirement plans, insurance benefits, seniority, paid vacations and holidays, sick days, Christmas bonuses, company cars, nice offices ... the list is nearly endless.

When I left the corporate world, I noticed that there was a lot of brainwashing going on.

Employees take great security in getting that one big income source without thinking about the glass foundation it sits on. That glass foundation is where you are dependent on one employer ... and you continue to labor. Indeed, the recent recession repeatedly delivered hard one-two blows to workers, laborers, and employees ... but people still cling to the notion of being an employee for life.

It is much like when you try to play with what appears to be a nice pit bull terrier ... but he turns around and bites you. You hurt and bleed for a while, and then you decide you will go find another pit bull to play with. But that pit bull also bites you and you hurt and bleed again. How many pit bulls will have to bite you before you realize that maybe you should stop playing with them altogether?

But I no longer talk about the ideas and concepts of money layers, expense layers, income layers, streaming income, perpetual wealth, personal freedom, time freedom, or monetary freedom to *disinterested* employees.

The reason why I won't waste my time and energy anymore is because:

"A blind man will not know what an ugly woman looks like."

This means that if you don't ever develop the ability to truly see, then you will never understand the problem. However, if you are reading this book, then you do not fall into the category of being *disinterested.*

I only talk with people who are interested in learning new ideas, a new lifestyle, meeting new people, and adopting alternative ways to view things.

As I said, employees want to talk about their salaries, benefits, vacation days, sick days, insurance plans, retirement plans, Christmas bonuses ... blah ... blah ... blah! All these things literally bore me, and they actually have little meaning to me nowadays.

What employees don't realize is that when you have the flexibility to sleep as late as you want or take time off almost anytime you want, you don't run around saying, "I can't wait until happy hour!" or "TGIF! Thank Goodness It's Friday! The weekend is here!" Any hour I choose is happy hour and every day is a weekend when I choose it.

The same thing with vacation pay, holiday pay, and sick days. These terms have very little meaning to me. The whole mindset behind them is that as an employee, you have periods of time during the year where you get paid even when you don't work. The reality for me is that when I take the vacation time and holidays I want off or when I am simply sick in bed, I get paid anyway. *The income layers I created pay me.* They are not "benefits" to me ... they are simply a part of my life and personal freedom.

When you have generated the appropriate income layers that can pay for your own insurance, insurance benefits tend to become less meaningful. Furthermore, when you have assets that continue to produce streaming income until old age, the notion of a company-sponsored retirement plan quickly loses its appeal.

I am not saying all this to be insulting or hurtful ... I say this because I am trying to make some very strong points here. For some people, old ideas and old habits die very, very hard. So the only way to break through is to sometimes be brutally direct and straightforward.

"People have been brainwashed in prison for so long that most of them have no idea what it's like to be outside the penitentiary."

One of the objectives in my writing this book was that only sincerely interested people and people of like-mind would be exposed to these "radical" ideas of mine. If you are an employee reading this book, please don't take offense because what I have said doesn't apply to you.

What I said doesn't apply to you because even though you may be an employee, you have spent your hard-earned dollars on this book ... and you have given your valuable time in order to read this far. This tells me that you are open-minded enough to accept alternative ideas. And why not?! If the old ideas were not working, why not try something new? It doesn't mean you have to agree with everything I say ... because in all reality ... we will have our own personal distinctions anyhow.

But remember the famous saying:

"The definition of insanity is to do the same thing and expect different results."

Don't you think it's time to try something new? I think so! And it begins by accepting new ideas and learning new things.

The Daily Grind

Because my parents were owners of a restaurant when I was young, and I often helped out behind the scenes by washing dishes, folding napkins, or wiping silverware, I was exposed to many types of people early on. There were the employees who came through ... as well as the customers. As I grew up, I began to notice many different things about people.

People of different ages seemed to pursue a life full of work and were constantly busy. In fact, there was all this talk of having a young man like myself looking forward to a life of going to school, then going to work in a career I would have to wisely decide on at an early age.

This message came through loud and clear ... repeatedly! Imagine my surprise several years later when I learned that people don't often work in the professions they studied for in school ... and not to mention that many of the courses taken by college students are frequently not used in the "real world."

What really disheartened me was the fact that so many people enrolled into a life of hard work, and they were continuously working in jobs they disliked until the age of retirement. When I glimpsed the future by watching the elderly, I actually saw a few who had in fact "made it." However, there were many more who lived diminished lives full of regret and fear of the remaining years they had left. These people discovered that the advice and the path they followed in their younger years did not work for them.

This created an early sense of unrest within me ... and it is partially why I spent most of my 20's driven to achieve and break the cycle of the future. Some people referred to their predicament as the "rat race of life" ... where people continue to run throughout their life. For me, I had a much more melodramatic view of it all. Today, I refer to it not as "running in the rat race" ... but as "grinding your life away" ... *mentally, physically, emotionally, and spiritually.*

Sometimes people refer to their daily tasks as part of their "daily grind." However, I refer to the lifestyle of unhappily working until old age to sustain your existence in society as the "grinding lifestyle."

The reason I refer to it as "grinding" is because of the long-term toll I have seen in people of all ages. It could be the single mother in her 20's toiling day in and day out to support her two children. It could be parents in their 40's who have created a lavish lifestyle that requires such heavy financial, physical, and psychological maintenance that they are tired and trapped inside ... but are afraid to let anyone know about it. Or it could be the elderly person who continues to work because their retirement is insufficient to support themselves - much less their medical needs.

Both the young and old grind away year in and year out until they become only a mere husk of the inner youthfulness that we all have within. The innocence is long gone ... and all that is left is a cynical person - a broken person full of regret and total lack of purpose.

Instead of working to create personal freedom and wealth for themselves and others, people continue to follow the old programming to work for a living, work to maintain their lifestyle of "looking good" to impress everyone ... and they sacrifice their futures along the way.

As I write this, it does not mean that I don't work. It does not mean I don't want to look good. However, what I am conscious of is that what I have built and continue to build allows for me to have a good amount of personal freedom ... where I can choose what I want to do and when I want to do it. Occasionally, I face the occasional grinding task, but I don't spend any more than two hours feeling strapped to any particular job or task. But I do have the freedom to break away or change what I want or need to at a moment's notice.

I am opposed to people spending their lives grinding away because I think all of us have the potential to become so much more than that. Most people have no time or wealth to possibly think about anything else ... yet they look forward to the next weekend where they can have a beer and watch a football or basketball game on television.

One of the biggest things I see with people trying to leave the daily grind is that they give the best time and energy that is available to their job. What happens is that they use any leftover energy and time in order to escape the daily grind.

I have transitioned from one career to another many times in my life. But during those times, I was able to use my spare time to successfully do so.

However, the leap from employee to self-employed or leaving one business to go into another business required me to take different measures. I used my spare time to do what I could to prepare myself for the transition.

Some people thought I worked too much. Well ... I called it "good planning."

The Emphasis on Professions

One huge problem is the way in which society places value on education. There is a great emphasis on white-collar professional education to learn skills needed on the job.

I see colleges offering curricula so that people can become engineers, accountants, doctors, attorneys, computer programmers, and so on. These students get led into curricula thinking that they are learning essential skills that will teach them to BECOME engineers, accountants, doctors, attorneys, and computer programmers.

But what people fail to realize is that college is often nothing more than a white-collar version of blue-collar vocational schools. *They are teaching people how to become employees with a profession ... not how to become a person that so many of us look for in others.* We look for people who are inspirational, empowering, motivational, wealthy, and famous ... and people who know how to make a big difference in the world.

There seems to be neither room nor priority within the college system that will allow someone to become inspirational, empowering, motivational, wealthy, or famous. These are not attributes that are necessarily encouraged in college ... but it is what we as people seek to become.

I would like to emphasize that there is nothing wrong with learning professional skills that allow you to contribute to society and make a living. However, I have learned through personal experience that we are not our professions and that we are not our jobs. It is simply something we do often for financial compensation. If people knew that, then they would not lose their self-identity when they lose their jobs or when they retire. Also, they wouldn't restrict themselves to doing only things they were formally educated to do.

I have heard many older people say that they would not know what they would do if they didn't have to work anymore. These people have confused what they do or what they did with who they are. Without their jobs, they feel that they would have little self-identity and self-worth.

We admire famous actors, outstanding athletes, talented musicians, philanthropists, authors, and greatly spiritual people. But why is that?

To the untrained eye and mind, we look only at the surface and material things ... such as the clothes they wear, the homes they live in, and the cars they drive. We also look at the places they visit and people they socialize with. Other people look heavily at what they have with only a casual thought of what they do.

Very little thought is used to think about what these people had to do *as individuals* in order to become a famous actor, outstanding athlete, or talented musician.

If you look at the history of many talented musicians, they had to work very hard and practice extensively behind the scenes for years ... often living very humbly and doing what they wanted to do for little or no pay. They talk about waiting on tables and playing in small clubs that provided little pay, and of course they also spent countless long hours to rehearse.

These people were not simply working for a living. These people were probably grinding by most peoples standards. However, they were working towards a dream ... by doing what it took to get there. By using their internal spirit and fortitude, they eventually overcame great odds and achieved the success and recognition they wanted.

The same goes for athletes. Many outstanding athletes gave up much of their normal childhood in order to perfect their skills and create the discipline needed to achieve the excellence they publicly display today. These people became great athletes as a result of their work on their internal spirit, self-determination, self-confidence, and discipline.

Unfortunately, very little of these internal qualities is formally taught.

Children Love to Play

When I watch children ... I realize they love life. Children want to play, explore, and experiment. They use lots of energy and simply go non-stop until they tire. Most of their existence is dedicated to playing, exploring, and having fun. I don't know any healthy children who would say that they would rather sit in a corner and do nothing. And yet we hear so many adults saying that every weekend!

As children grow into teenagers, they almost always want to do something ... whether it is eating, dancing, going out with friends, playing sports, talking on the phone, dating, reading, playing videogames, watching movies, and so on. Teenagers want to play, too! They may be older than small children ... but teenagers fundamentally still want to play; they want to explore, and they want to have new experiences.

I simply do not see healthy teenagers volunteering or wanting to go into their rooms to do "absolutely nothing." It simply does not happen. But on the other hand, many adults repeat that very sentiment each and every day.

As people grow into adults, they somehow have to learn to fend for themselves and they must be responsible for their own well-being. They get themselves into bad relationships, bad jobs, bad credit, and bad situations ... and then life seems to take over.

They find themselves in situations they cannot get out of, and taking on responsibilities they don't always want. Furthermore, because most of their time is spent doing things they don't want to do, their lives no longer have any playtime. All the play in their adult lives has disappeared ... and it inevitably becomes work ... hard work ... grinding away.

It has been said that the difference between men and boys are simply the size and cost of their toys. You know ... there is a certain amount of truth to this. Because just like boys, men want to play, too. In fact, both men and women like to play. Even as adults, people want to play. People will ALWAYS want to play ... no matter how young or old they are.

The problem is that most of the healthy forms of play is taken out for adults. Some forms of unhealthy play for adults might include drinking, smoking, gambling, and deviant sex. Healthier forms of adult play might include sports, travel, sex, socializing, collecting, and so on.

The main issue with the way people work today is that they are not playing ... they are simply grinding. People have been taught that if they are being productive, then it cannot be looked upon as "play-time."

However, that is not true. We only need to look at Sam Walton, Bill Gates, Warren Buffett, Michael Dell, and other billionaires that continue to work despite having all the money and time in the world.

The fact is ... *they are doing what they want in life.* They are doing big things ... and making huge changes in the world. The money and wealth they have is not enough to get them to quit. They want to play ... and they want to continue on playing.

Instead of thinking about a way to retire and do nothing, I think that it is probably healthier to find more ways to play … and make your work a form of play.

Some of my friends have asked why I don't play as many games as I did before. I simply reply, "Why would I play board games or computer games when I can play it in real life?"

I don't need to play Monopoly© or Easy Money© when I can do business and real estate deals in real life! I don't need to go to Las Vegas to gamble my money away when I can use my money in business and investing activities where my odds are much better … and where I have some control over the rules and conditions of the game.

When I launch a new business venture or make a new real estate investment, it is like starting a new game where I create the rules.

Many of the games I used to play in my teens and 20's I now play in real life. And as such, most days are fun and full of challenge for me.

The Fallacy of Retirement

So many people are looking forward to retirement! They are all looking forward to the day when they have finally saved up enough money in order to comfortably grow old and do nothing.

I have never understood that type of thinking. And yet when I look at the way in which so many people live their lives, I begin to understand *why* they think that way.

Some of the people I see lead what I consider to be rather tragic lives.

There are people who are married to spouses who they don't really want to be married to, they have children they never planned on having, and they steadily work in jobs they hate. Furthermore, when they have any time off, their time and energy is usually spent on taking care of things they have to take care of.

They are always broke, they feel the world is conspiring against them, and they feel that the government should do more for them.

These people don't live their lives, but instead life seems to happen to them. It is one tragic story after another. And the little pleasure they have seems to come from gossiping and spending their weekends drinking beer.

The picture I described does not apply to every person, but I would venture to guess that there are parts of that picture that apply to many people.

What the picture centers on is the issue that so many people are spending time with people they don't care to be with and doing things they would rather not do. They are running around based on what everyone tells them they should do instead of trying to take control of their lives. They have no time, no energy ... and no inspiration.

It is no wonder then why so many people dream of the day they will retire!

In my own life, I have worked hard, played hard, and yes ... I have also rested hard. What does "rested hard" mean? It means that I have taken the opportunity to simply do nothing except relax, think, and indulge myself during different periods of my life.

Several years ago, when I resigned my position from what would be my last full-time employer, I told myself that after steadily working and going to school for nearly ten years, I would take a sabbatical. How long would that be? I didn't know at the time, but I knew I wanted more than just a mere two weeks off to simply reflect on life and try to figure out which direction I wanted to travel.

One late summer afternoon, I got into my well-used little Honda Accord, pulled out of my parking space, and drove away from the employee parking lot for the last time. That was my last day of work ... and I did NOT look back.

Although I was relieved to go, part of me was also sad. I was saying good-bye to the place where I had worked for nearly three years ... and it was with a company that had provided me the seasoning and maturity I needed to tackle new opportunities.

As I drove down the highway, a feeling of complete freedom suddenly washed over me. I knew I had no commitments to anyone anymore ... except to myself. I had few responsibilities and very little to hold me back. I kept thinking to myself, "Okay. Now what do I do?"

While I was not monetarily free, I had the means to live conservatively for nearly a year without having to worry about working. I would like to say that it was because I had a ton of money saved up ... but that wasn't the case at all. All I had were two brand new credit lines that were established before I resigned.

I boldly told my family and friends that I had no intentions of doing anything. I was going to indulge myself by sleeping when I wanted ... and however late I wanted. I was not going to work on anything professionally related. I was simply going "to be" and enjoy my freedom.

At the time, I thought that my opportunity to do "absolutely nothing" was going to be only a rare occurrence in my life. But I based that assumption on my observations on how everyone else seemed to live their lives: busy, complicated ... and full of drama.

I figured I had better take this opportunity to "do nothing" because I didn't know when that opportunity would come up again.

And so, for the next two weeks, I did exactly that: *nothing*. Absolutely zilch ... nada ... zero. I have to admit that I was quite the unproductive person ... and proudly so I might add. I secretly chuckled to myself that while everyone had to go to work and faced a ton of responsibilities - here I was enjoying myself with very little time commitments.

One day, during my quiet time of reflection, I thought of what I might want to do after I came out of my sabbatical. Having gained a lot of field and business experience and recently graduated with a Master's Degree, I thought it might be interesting to see what opportunities there were in teaching.

It was actually quite ironic! For so many years I hated attending classes; it seemed like such a chore going to night classes year after year. But now that I had completed my graduate degree, I began to wonder how much greener the grass might be on the other side of the classroom.

I got my phone book out and looked up the phone numbers of the local community colleges ... and placed some exploratory calls. Well, what turned out to be an exploratory call turned out to be an *interview* call! Apparently, in my casual reference of my graduate degree, field experience, and technical certifications, the Program Manager I spoke to wanted to hire me. In fact, he wanted to know when I could come in so that he could meet me in person! Apparently, he had been looking for additional adjunct professors to fill the fall semester ... of which I found out was only three weeks away. So ... in the end I agreed to meet him the following day.

During our meeting, he asked if I was interested in the position. And despite the fact that I was still on sabbatical ... I agreed to it.

When I returned home, I received a message from the other major community college that they too were interested in interviewing me. I found out they also needed additional faculty for some night courses. After submitting an application, resume, and going through the interview process, I was hired as an adjunct professor for them as well!

I had to chuckle to myself. I went from resigning from the corporate world with no plan of action to taking a sabbatical. After only three weeks of sabbatical, I was going to be back in the workforce ... doing something I never imagined I would do. Being a long time student, I would now have the opportunity to become a teacher. I would celebrate my 29th birthday by becoming an adjunct college professor for two community colleges.

Why have I told you this story?

I have told you this story because there were some lessons I learned during this "retirement period."

I realized it was very difficult to do absolutely nothing. Sure, I enjoyed lounging and wandering around as I saw fit. I got to watch plenty of television, played on the computer, read casually, slept late, and talked on the phone. But in the end, doing absolutely nothing became rather boring.

It was this boredom that led me to imagine and play with different possibilities ... which then in turn eventually led to my making those exploratory phone calls.

I also realized that when I had plenty of time, I could take advantage of great opportunities that came up. Because I had no commitments to anyone else, I was free to accept both instructor positions at both community colleges.

Since then, I have had other opportunities to give myself mini-sabbaticals and mini-retirement experiences. And each time, I would feel refreshed and rejuvenated ... but always ready to take on something new.

In fact, the book that you are reading today emerged as an idea from one of my mini-sabbaticals. As a result, I have been excited about writing and publishing this book. And while certain aspects of writing and publishing this book have been work (and even grueling at times), it has largely been an enlightening experience and a labor of love.

I have come to the conclusion that people who have never experienced a sabbatical or mini-retirement ... where their time and destiny is their own (even if it is for a short period of time) ... they have no concept of what "doing nothing" truly means. It simply means you eat, drink, sleep ... and breathe to live. Everything else is truly optional. But it is also extremely boring and completely uninspiring ... but it does allow you the time to reflect on where you are and where you might want to go.

The 10-Hour Work Week

People throughout American history have longed for the day when the 40-hour workweek would be reduced to thirty hours.

And you know ... there actually was a time when that seemed to be a growing reality. After all, with all the advancements of automation and computer technology, surely the need for people would be reduced.

The fact is people are more productive than ever with automation and computers. However, what people failed to realize was that with the increased efficiency, each person would be called upon to take on more responsibility. In effect, this would cancel out any realized gains from automation and technology in terms of recuperating their time.

There is a saying that "nature abhors a vacuum." The natural tendency of increased efficiency for employers is not to reduce the work hours for an employee and give them the same pay ... they give them *more* to do in the *same amount of time* for the *same* pay.

What most employees don't understand is that no matter how productive and efficient they become, they will never be able to substantially reduce the number of hours they have to work. Like our culture says: you are either working full-time, part-time, or no-time.

Work by an employee is still fundamentally measured by how many hours they put in ... and not necessarily how productive and efficient they are.

Even people who are self-employed are trained to work at least forty hours a week. If they work less than that then they start to feel guilty.

When I made these observations, I knew I could no longer follow conventional wisdom. I had to create a new way of thinking for myself. I would have to redesign my life.

Because I focused on creating income layers and the amount of work was generally minimal in maintaining them, I quickly realized that as I got smarter and more experienced,

I could actually live a 10-hour work week. And as a matter of fact, I often did! I spent the rest of my time reading, attending seminars and workshops, writing this book, thinking, planning, and exploring new business opportunities.

Now, there may be some people who might say, "Why not go for having a zero-hour workweek?" The reason why that is not an attractive goal for me is because there is a point of diminishing return to reduce it to zero hours. The effort it would take to not participate in any aspect of my livelihood would in effect put me in a position of once again being a dependent ... by letting everyone make every single financial decision for me.

When you consider that there are 168 hours per week – out of which I have to work only ten of them (or less than 6% of my week), that doesn't sound too bad to me.

Or when I compare it to people working 40 to 60 hours per week, having the ability to work only ten hours comes very close to retirement. After all, do I work two hours per day for five days, and then have a standard two-day weekend? Do I work 2.5 hours per day for four days and have a three-day weekend? Or do I work nearly 3.5 hours per day for three days and have a four-day weekend?

Do you see what I mean? None of these sound very painful to me. A 10-hour workweek is simply not that demanding for anyone.

When I only have to work ten hours per week to maintain my lifestyle, the notion of holiday pay, sick pay, and vacation pay ... it all means very little to me. These things only matter to employees because they have so little control of their time. These things are their tokens of comfort ... in knowing that their financial needs will be met while they are not working during those times. However, it is mostly an illusion.

I would like to point out that while I can get away with working only ten hours per week (and I occasionally do during times when I don't feel well or when I simply feel a need for a break), I generally don't.

The biggest reason is that there are many more things I want to accomplish in my life with the surplus time I have created. I would much rather find more constructive and productive things to do with my time than simply watching television, getting drunk, getting high, or just doing nothing.

Like I said in an earlier chapter, people who simply want to retire and do nothing are probably the least likely to ever achieve personal freedom in their lifetimes ... and it is mainly due to their own laziness.

Isn't it ironic that the people who want to retire and do nothing the most are the people least likely to ever achieve it? Furthermore, the people who are most able to create their personal freedom will likely accomplish more in their lives than the people who work full-time at a job and dream about personal freedom.

These may be broad generalizations, but I have often found this to be true. I spend a little over ten hours of my week maintaining my existing lifestyle. I spend the other 30+ hours improving, enhancing, and expanding my own and other people's lifestyles.

There is a difference between working full-time to maintain your lifestyle (which I see most people doing) and working full-time to continue building and improving your own and other people's lifestyle. The difference is how many lives you can touch and affect.

This book is a prime example of this. As an author, my lifestyle stands to improve if book sales are good. Not only that, if this book does in fact sell well; where it makes an impact on you and teaches you some new ideas and insights, then I hope in some small way I have improved your life. That in itself would be very gratifying to me.

Even in my own real estate investing, as my portfolio grows (because I have more properties to sell), I bring more opportunities to people who wish to become homeowners. But there are also more investors that I serve by becoming larger.

The larger I become, the more people I serve to make a difference in their lives.

Taking it another step further, if my online businesses continue to grow and prosper, I am much more able to share the wealth I have earned to create more income opportunities for others.

By creating more personal freedom for myself, the more I can serve others and provide value. I have more time and resources to focus on larger problems and challenges that go beyond myself. The problem with working as an employee is that you are working full-time primarily to support your existing lifestyle ... which is often more than what you can handle.

As people progress in creating their personal freedom, I highly recommend that they begin to reduce the amount of time they spend in maintaining their lifestyles ... and increase their time in order to serve others ... whether it is their family, children, neighborhood, or community.

Even if maintaining your personal freedom required twenty hours a week, you would have cut back the amount of time you had to work in half when compared to most employees. Most employees would be ecstatic if they only had to work twenty hours a week to support themselves.

In a family household, where there is a husband and wife, if each of them only had to work ten hours a week to maintain their lifestyle, would they not have more time to spend with their children and each other? Could they not use the remainder of their time to improve their family's lifestyle?

The options and opportunities open up when you can have personal freedom to the point where you only have to work ten hours a week in order to maintain your income layers. I believe the idea of a 10-hour workweek is a worthwhile goal to work towards.

Where Are Your Best Hours Going?

I geared up to walk away from my technology training business years ago. It was my plan to build up my income layers as replacement income while I phased out of my training business.

As such, I spent a lot of time reading and studying ... trying to learn new habits and skills for my future life. I also wanted to be well versed in the real estate investing I planned on doing. Although I was fairly knowledgeable in some aspects of real estate (having been exposed to it for many years already), I worked on building up an array of specialized knowledge that I could draw on. It did not mean that I had to know everything or was trying to be an expert in everything. It simply meant that if I developed a mental toolkit for myself, I would be better prepared to deal with different situations as they arose.

As I studied and planned, I became proactive in re-orienting my financial position. This meant looking at all my resources and options. I evaluated my credit and debt position, I looked at the expenses I would be incurring, and so on. I shut down accounts that did not serve me well and opened new accounts that were more favorable. I shifted some of my debt, as well as my available funds, into more favorable positions.

With the meticulous planning and scrutiny I went through, you would have thought I was going to war. And actually, when I think about it ... I suppose I was! I was going to war to win my personal freedom once and for all. I was willing to take a lot of personal and financial risk to win my personal freedom. It was a fight I intended to win.

Because I was already in my early 30's, it was not in my best interests to postpone this course of action. Unlike so many people I have known ... they believed that their 30's was not the best time to start. I thought to myself, "Well then ... when exactly *is* the best time?" They believed that during this time you are just getting established and are finally attaining a level of respect that wasn't reached earlier.

My question was, "Is waiting until you are in your 40's or 50's any easier?" I think that waiting until you are in your 40's and 50's is actually much more risky. The chances of successful recovery diminish if something goes wrong. Furthermore, most people in their 40's and 50's actually become more fearful ... not more courageous.

In any case, I quickly learned not to debate with those who are fundamentally paralyzed with fear, paranoia, cynicism, and negativity. It doesn't matter what you say to them because they have lost the battle within their minds even before it has begun. I believe that they have guaranteed themselves a life of mediocrity ... where they will have to work until old age.

As I set out to create a streaming line of income, I found the process somewhat slow in the beginning. I largely attributed it to me having to travel in my contract training business. During the week before I had to leave, I would scramble to leave my projects at a good stopping point ... just so that I could leave. When I did leave town, I left for a week and could not accomplish anything while I was gone. When I finally returned, I would be exhausted. I would spend another few days just to recover from my trip and catch up on things. In effect, a one-week business trip took away two weeks of my time for working on building my income layers.

To make matters worse, the two weeks downtime actually created disruption in my workflow and loss of momentum. So, it would seem each month would pass by and very little got accomplished.

The insight that I later got was that I was giving the best hours of my time to someone else and giving myself the leftovers. When I looked back to my days as an employee, I discovered the same thing. People give the best hours of their day to their employers or someone else. The remaining or leftover time is then used for their projects and personal time.

This realization made me even more discontent. As I worked to serve my clients in my business, I found that the most important project ... my personal freedom ... was taking a back seat. I was using my best time and energy for clients and a business I had lost interest in. Meanwhile, I was using leftover time and energy to work on the most important project of my life. Somehow that made no sense to me ... and I had a great urgency to correct this.

As a cautionary note, what follows is not a recommendation for anyone to do! I am simply sharing what I did with you, not necessarily what you should do. It is extremely risky and can have some seriously negative consequences!

As I mentioned earlier, I decided to quit my business "cold turkey." Not only did I put myself in a position of no income, I also outwardly announced to everyone that I was leaving my career of ten years in the information technology business ... and stressed to them that I would never go back. In effect, I intentionally burned my bridges. I did this because, in the event of failure, I would have "egg on my face" if I did try to go back. The intent was to set myself up so that I had no choice but to move forward ... and ultimately succeed.

Looking back, it was quite risky what I did. But my emotional need to leave that life and the confines of what most employees and self-employed people go through was extremely high. My belief was that if I could achieve my personal freedom ... even at a temporarily reduced lifestyle ... it would be well worth it. Then, when I had my personal freedom, I could work on improving my lifestyle.

It is obvious by now that I did in fact succeed and achieve a level of personal freedom I currently enjoy otherwise I would not and could not have the time to write this book. But as I tell my personal story and advise people, I strongly remind them that I had taken an enormous financial risk by quitting cold turkey ... yet I had also done a great deal of preparation beforehand.

My position is that people should study, practice, and build some income layers *before* they abandon their current income sources ... even if it is a full-time job as an employee.

Your time is precious, and I think that it's very important for people to achieve personal freedom for themselves.

But without being aware of the fact that most people give the best hours of their lives to their employers and others – and ultimately giving themselves the leftover time when they are more exhausted and least inspired, you can't make the effort to shift and reorient your life. You need to change things where you give *yourself* the best hours and energy... not your employers or other people.

You Will Leave One Way or Another!

There is never any question about whether you will leave your current job or business. *You will leave one way or another* ... it is simply a question of *HOW* and *WHEN*. But unfortunately, rather than making this decision for themselves, the majority of people leave it for others to decide.

In the old days, people stayed with the same company and only left the workforce when they reached the age of retirement and received their pensions. This is what many people would still like to have happen, but unfortunately, this is no longer realistic.

I remember in the mid-1990's when both AT&T and IBM announced they were laying people off. It had been widely publicized ... so it was not just a rumor. And as most large companies did, they offered incentives and severance packages to those that would willingly leave. There were people who saw the writing on the wall and understood what was going to happen.

People within the "first wave" who immediately took the severance packages often found them quite generous. During the "second wave," there were incentives and severance packages as well ... but definitely not as generous as those that occurred in the first wave. This continued on to the point where very little was given. The people towards the end chose to hang on as long as they could - but the axe fell anyway and they got nothing for being the last ones out the door.

The problem was, despite the financial incentives provided by the companies, the people towards the end could not mentally or emotionally give up their seniority, pension packages, and benefits. Ultimately, the decision that was rightfully theirs to make was taken over and chosen for them. Those that stayed behind were left with the cleanup and they had to deal with all the low morale. In my eyes, that is not a great reward either.

I am not encouraging people to irresponsibly abandon their jobs, employers, or businesses. I am simply stating that there are often general indicators of impending change. We can either embrace the change and find opportunities ... or we can let it all happen to us and become victims of it.

We generally have choices available. Personally, I have always made it a policy to make exits on my terms and generally on a high note ... not when things were at their worst with things crashing down all around me.

People need to realize that one way or another they will leave the job or business they are currently in. They can choose when ... or it can be chosen for them.

The Importance of Time

Much of what I have created in my life involves realizing the importance of my time, the desire for time freedom and effective time utilization. I know of no better way to illustrate this to you than by sharing with you two simple anonymously-written articles I found on the Internet. There seem to be many variations of these two articles. Since they are apparently in the public domain, I have taken creative liberties to re-adapt some of the words and passages for better impact.

I hope you enjoy these as I have. I remember these each and every day.

Imagine A Bank...
By Unknown Writer

Imagine there is a bank that credits your account each morning with $86,400, it carries over no balance from one day to the next, and every evening it deletes whatever part of the balance you failed to use. What would you do? Draw out every cent of course!

Each of us has such a bank – and its name is TIME. Whether you are the richest man on the planet or the poorest, it makes no difference. Every morning, you are credited with 86,400 seconds. Every night it completely writes off the balance you have failed to use towards good purposes. It also doesn't carry over a balance, and it allows absolutely no overdraft.

Each day it opens a new account for you, and each night it burns the remains of the day. If you fail to use that day's deposits, the loss is yours. There is no going back. There is no drawing against the "tomorrow."

You must live in the present on today's deposits. Invest it wisely in order to get the utmost in health, happiness, freedom, and success from it! The clock is running. Make the most of today and everyday!

The Value of Time

By Unknown writer (Portions revised by Matthew Chan)

✓ To realize the value of ONE YEAR, ask a student who failed a grade.

✓ To realize the value of ONE MONTH, ask a mother who gave birth to a premature baby.

✓ To realize the value of ONE WEEK, ask a writer of a weekly newspaper.

✓ To realize the value of ONE DAY, ask an applicant who missed a job interview.

✓ To realize the value of ONE HOUR, ask the lovers who are waiting to meet.

✓ To realize the value of ONE MINUTE, ask the person who just missed his plane.

✓ To realize the value of ONE SECOND, ask the soldier's wife whose phone just stopped ringing.

✓ To realize the value of ONE MILLISECOND, ask the racecar driver who came in 2nd place.

The Intrepid Way

5 | Entrepreneurial Mindset

Becoming an Entrepreneur

One of my early ambitions and aspirations as a young man was that I would one day become a CEO of some large company. Today, in light of all the corporate scandals, such as Enron, Arthur Andersen ... and too many others to mention, the very title of CEO has lost its luster and prestige. Nevertheless, the CEO often represents the chief principal of a company.

The idea of being a leader of a large company that did great things had always appealed to me. And although being paid well was an attraction to becoming a CEO, my need to be recognized, have influence, have the ability to make an everlasting impact, and doing large things was greater.

I once had a conversation with Judy whose family and company I briefly worked for. I shared my ambitions with her that I wanted to one day become a CEO of a large company. Because I had gone to the same junior high school as her daughter, she seemed to treat me in a more personal and nurturing way than a normal employer-employee relationship. This is what she told me:

"The quickest way to become the CEO of a company is to one day start your own company."

I have never forgotten that piece of impacting advice. What she was actually saying was that I would eventually have to become an entrepreneur just like her husband did.

I believe too many people feel that they have to get "permission" from someone else to progress and grow, and that this "higher" someone has to give them authorization to do great things. The fact is, you don't in the world of entrepreneurship and capitalism. If you have products, services, and ideas that people want, sometimes that is all you need to get started.

I don't refer to myself as a CEO now because it has too many negative and large corporate connotations. Regardless of the title, I have chosen to be proactive and take charge of my own life, my company, and the projects I take on to make a difference for my business partners, investors, customers, and myself. *Anyone* can become a CEO and have their own little company if they are willing to step outside the circle and simply say so. You do not need to be "promoted" within some corporate structure in order to advance or grow.

If you do well by people, you will simply be recognized and elevated upwards by the marketplace ... and not by some appointed or hired authority figure either.

In fact, this book is self-published because I didn't feel the need to ask a publisher if this book was of value to them. I figured I would write and publish it ... then turn it loose into the marketplace and let my customers tell me themselves if it was really worth it.

I had to be willing to say to myself, "I want to become a published author and have the opportunity to share my message. What is the fastest way I can do this?" For me, it was not writing a book proposal or shopping it around with various publishers or agents. It was to start writing it, getting it edited, getting a cover designed, and <u>then</u> get it printed.

All it took was for me to decide. Likewise, all it takes is for you to decide.

Entrepreneurial Spirit

The entrepreneurial spirit is the fire behind every entrepreneur, and it generally epitomizes the emotional side of us. It is the drive to create, accomplish, achieve, and initiate. It is the spark that allows a fire to start. It is the inner drive and motivation to create a business to serve others.

Entrepreneurship is more appropriately referred to as "opportuneurship."

Entrepreneurs seek out and find opportunities. But opportunities are seen within the mind ... not with the eyes. Taking the action to capitalize on those opportunities requires this entrepreneurial spirit.

I believe that everyone have some degree of entrepreneurial spirit within them. But whether that potential is ultimately developed is inversely related to the person's tolerance of risk and change.

The greater the entrepreneurial spirit, the greater the willingness to take risks, accept change, and the need for control over one's destiny. Entrepreneurs often want to be leaders and be responsible for their own destinies ... not dependent on others to create their destinies for them.

People who have lower levels of entrepreneurial spirit tend to value security, low change, and low risk. Control over one's destiny and personal freedom is secondary to them having security.

Ironically, in today's economy it is the true entrepreneurs who are coping better than the employees. Because in a world of layoffs, downsizing, bankruptcies, and scandal, employees have little control and even fewer options. The nature of entrepreneurs is that they are responsible for their financial income and bringing in business; whereas employees are heavily dependent on convincing an employer to provide them their livelihood.

People in labor unions team up to force company managements to provide more for them. It's a shame really that they don't put the same team effort into creating opportunities for themselves *outside* of the company.

The two main fuels that make businesses burn are the *entrepreneurial spirit* and *opportunity*. When the two fuels are combined, spectacular fires begin to burn ... and results are seen and success is accomplished.

Opportunity

Opportunity is the thought or perception that great benefits can be cultivated and derived through work. It has been said, "One man's dog is another man's opportunity."

One of the fatal flaws that many beginning entrepreneurs make is that they continue the mentality of "employeeship," where they provide direct labor in exchange for direct pay.

Many self-employed entrepreneurs continue this tradition. This is why when they stop working their income quickly goes away or the amount of time they put in is directly tied to their financial well-being. The only difference is that they charge higher fees or hourly rates.

However, more sophisticated entrepreneurs create or seek to control and capture the opportunity to receive multiple payoffs.

Working for the Opportunity

As I said before, it's easy to simply work for a living ... and there is nothing wrong with doing so. However, after years of exchanging direct labor for direct pay, I found it too limiting and restrictive for me. I did not see it as an easy path to gain personal freedom or financial security.

I eventually realized that it was simply not that hard to work at some job for a living. All I had to do was simply be frugal and exercise some good money habits. And for retirement, I had to keep socking the leftover money away, hope that I saved enough, and pray that my investments would grow fast enough.

I never felt good about the plan ... but that was all I knew. It would not be until after I completed my Master's Degree and realized that nothing significantly changed that I realized the answers were not in any college or with any large company I could work for.

For the last few years, I have chosen to work for personal freedom. By having personal freedom, it allows me the time and financial means to pursue what makes me happy and personally fulfilled.

In Chapter 2, I gave you a financial roadmap of how I created perpetual wealth ... how I gradually built one layer at a time in order to "set me free." My model was based on understanding the *Money Layers* ... by creating, building, and managing income layers that ultimately exceed my expense layers.

Not only did I have to change the "rules of money" in my mind, I also had to change the way I created value and did business.

As I said earlier, the entrepreneurial spirit seeks out opportunity. You become a student of "opportuneurship."

Most people work in a direct exchange of their time and efforts for money in a limited income model. When I worked as a technology instructor, I often got paid $125 per hour on a contract basis. Although by most people's standards that is a good hourly pay, *it was still limited.* Once I earned and received payment for the work I put in, there was no more income. There was no residual income or benefits afterwards.

Because of this lack of residual benefits, people have to get back on that treadmill to once again directly generate the pay. This repetition is what causes people to have to work fully ... week after week ... their entire lifetimes. This I truly feel can actually make some people grow old before their time.

For me, I knew I had to break that cycle of direct work for direct pay. What I began working for was <u>not</u> direct pay. I noticed that very successful people often worked for gaining the larger opportunity than the one-time payoff.

I define "working for the opportunity" as work for the following reasons:

- To showcase my abilities and talents.

- To establish or build my credibility.

- To create an educational or learning experience.

- To establish or further my track record.

- To expand my network of contacts.

- To showcase my ability to be a leader, take responsibility and accept consequences.

- To showcase my ability to be a team player and work within a team for the larger opportunity.

- To show my willingness to set aside my ego and need for quick financial compensation for the larger opportunity.

- To demonstrate my commitment and convictions in the people and causes I work for.

- To prove my willingness to personally risk my reputation and personal resources to attain the larger opportunity.

- To create, cultivate, or strengthen a relationship, friendship, or alliance.

- To create a greater benefit and value so that everyone could benefit.

I stopped working directly for money, and I started working for the overall opportunity ... which was more valuable in the long run than any short-term money I could ever earn.

What I discovered was that working for the opportunity quite often created much larger rewards.

I also found that there was a compounding effect: the more success I had in working for the opportunity, the more rewards I received financially. I found that creating opportunities was easy when I used a very simple formula: *work to create goodwill!*

I followed a mantra from the movie, "The Godfather", where Marlon Brando boldly said,

"I made them an offer they couldn't refuse."

As I said before, most people will not work for free because their paradigm says that you do not work unless you get money. By consciously breaking that paradigm, and being willing to give my own time and resources to someone else, it was not hard to stand out among the crowd, get noticed, and be presented with opportunities.

"Working for small opportunities can reveal larger opportunities."

This does not mean that well-established entrepreneurs do not want to get paid. It simply means they take longer-term view of business. By capturing the opportunity, multiple benefits and paydays emerge.

Entrepreneurs Go Beyond Themselves

One thing I notice about people who work for others is that they focus most on what they can see, touch, and predict.

Employees generally focus on what is guaranteed and the benefits they can quantify. They generally require a predictable income.

An entrepreneur's general focus is on opportunity, service, and creating value. Good entrepreneurs think of income as potentially limitless.

People are not taught to see and recognize opportunity. Nor are they taught to create opportunity!

Entrepreneurs create opportunity and have a vision in their minds. What they then do is take those visions ... and through work, creativity, and ingenuity manage to manifest them into reality.

People who are not entrepreneurs tend to simply depend on the value of their direct labor. The problem is that there is a limit to how much value one person can deliver if you are focused only on your work.

Entrepreneurs do in fact work and put in their time and labor. However, it is often done at the starting point to launch an idea, project, or venture. They then build on top of that by finding new efficiencies by actively look for technology, additional employees, business relationships, investors, financing, and so on to further their growth.

They are willing to go beyond themselves.

Employees don't often look beyond themselves to create value. They may use computers, tools, equipment, and so forth ... but it is almost always in the context of simply doing more within forty hours a week, and not necessarily with the goal of doing less.

The entrepreneurial spirit requires you to look and go beyond yourself. It forces you to not only look at what you want, but also to be aware of what others want.

Putting Your Stake in the Ground

One of my favorite movies is, "Far and Away," starring Tom Cruise and Nicole Kidman. I know that hecklers of the movie mock it because of Tom Cruise's portrayal of an Irish immigrant. I have heard that Tom's version of an Irish accent is less than accurate, but nevertheless I still enjoyed the movie.

The movie was about an Irishman who wanted to come to the United States and claim a small piece of opportunity for himself. Tom's character immigrated into the United States to participate in the land rush of the late 1800's. In the movie, Tom's character was a poor but ambitious man ... all he wanted was a chance to establish himself.

The U.S. government was giving away divided plots of land, and he wanted to fairly claim a piece of land to call his own. All he had to do was show up at a predetermined place and time and participate in a race to claim his title of land. The way to get his piece of land was to be the first person to get to whichever plot of land he desired and put his wooden stake into the ground to mark it.

As you might guess from a Hollywood movie, Tom's character, with great drama and heroism, did in fact succeed in placing a wooden stake on a piece of land ... with of course some help from Nicole Kidman's character.

I see so much opportunity in the world today, yet so few people are able or willing to put their stakes in the ground. In fact, there is so much opportunity ... I often put multiple stakes in the ground.

So many people think it takes a lot of money to put a stake in the ground. But the reality of it is that sometimes it doesn't. One of the largest opportunities I see is on the Internet. For only a $15 domain registration fee, people can claim a small piece of digital real estate for themselves. To activate that piece of digital real estate costs less than $20 per month to reach the world market.

Other examples I see are the large networks already established by Amazon.com, Yahoo.com, and ebay.com. It costs nearly nothing to reach the world market today. All it takes to begin is to say, "Yes, I am willing to put my stake in the ground."

These are not the only ways to put your stake in the ground though. Another way I have put my stake in the ground is by buying many smaller investment properties that now produce streaming income for me. And because I have done it successfully many times, I attract others who want to put my stakes in the ground with me.

There are practically no limits to how many stakes you can put into the ground. But it starts with the willingness to do so ... and then learning how to grow what you have claimed.

After all, most of the great structures of the world began with an idea, a piece of blank paper, and an empty plot of land. There are all kinds of land available today ... including the digital kind.

Yellow Lights & Red Lights

I often run into skeptics telling me things that they can't do, why things will fail for them, why things won't work, and basically argue the case on how they will not win or succeed.

I have run into others that say, "If someone would give me the answer or show me how to do it, I could fix my problems." Unfortunately, those people will be disappointed for the rest of their lives because there is no "one specific answer" to becoming wealthy and personally free.

They never go anywhere because they get so caught up and concerned in the details. This reminds me of a saying I once heard, *"People are waiting for every traffic light to become green before they will get out and drive. This is why they never go anywhere."* If you are waiting for all "green lights," that day may never come. You will inevitably run into "yellow lights" and "red lights" in any journey you try to pursue.

Intellectuals and experts pride themselves on their knowledge and expert skills. They immediately assume that if they cannot figure it out, then it cannot be done.

I have a friend who is multi-talented ... where one of his talents is having the ability to build unique furniture. He frequently gets glowing comments from friends and visitors.

"What a unique design." "Very contemporary."

People have offered to pay him to make furniture ... but he declines every time. He vowed for many years that he did not want his hobby to become work ... as he equated work with displeasure. In my view, if working within my "hobby" happens to make me money, I am ecstatic. In his mind, he was not allowed to profit from it ... even when he had potential customers waiting.

But eventually he did begin to accept that perhaps there might be some way to leverage his talents in woodwork and furniture into making some money.

I told him "Great! It would be a natural fit for you!"

But unfortunately, he automatically dismissed making the furniture all these people wanted and simply wanted to pursue the idea and design of it.

He surmised that it was not reasonable because his furniture was too complex to manufacture cost-effectively. While that may be true, I told him why not have someone else see if **they** could find a way to make it happen? He did not believe it because **he** could not figure it out. He automatically assumed no one else could.

While I encouraged him to pursue the furniture business and perhaps position it as an elite product that would allow for lower volume production and higher pricing, he automatically compared it to furniture from **Rooms to Go**. He wrongfully assumed that everyone price-shopped aggressively just because he is that way.

He is one of thousands of people who have good ideas but are unable to implement or even attempt it. They think it is the idea that is the value ... when in reality it is the *implementation* that makes the difference in our world. And his thought was if he couldn't figure out a way to implement it with his engineering degree, no one else could.

If everyone thought like that, we would never have put a man on the moon or launched the space shuttle. The fact is not one person will have enough brainpower to figure the entire process out if the project is large.

How Big is Your Playground?

After I graduated high school and tried to prepare myself for the world of college (and ultimately the corporate world), I heard of businessmen traveling around the country to different cities - staying in nice hotels and eating in nice restaurants in order to conduct business.

There was something glamorous about the idea of being important enough for some company to pay travel expenses just to have you present for some sort of business deal. Not to mention the fact that you were doing a job that was not so mundane ... where you had to be confined to an office.

In fact, it wasn't until about six years later that I had to travel for business in the Southeast U.S. Unfortunately, it was not quite as glamorous as I had imagined. I did fly ... but it was coach ... not first class. I stayed at a hotel ... but it was a Holiday Inn ... not the Hyatt. I ate at restaurants ... but it was often at a 24-hour Denny's or Perkins ... not at a more upscale Steak & Ale. Certainly not the glitz and glamour I had dreamed about, but it was still a fun experience for me at the time.

What I found interesting were the subtle differences of the local people; the way they lived, where they worked, and how they spent their time. I also noticed how every city

I visited was quite different ... but at the same time also similar in some ways.

Every city and town had their own streets, landmarks, downtowns, lakes, governments, and businesses. However, what I also noticed was there were Wal-Marts, K-Marts, McDonalds, Burger Kings, Red Lobster's, Olive Gardens, and other recognizable brand name chain businesses.

I also noticed there was a downtown in the city's center, as well as suburbs in the outer sections of the city. There were major highways and streets that would run north-south and east-west. There were the rougher parts of town and there were the more affluent parts of town. And while the appearance and actual layout was different from city to city, overall I did see recognizable patterns.

And while there were some subtle differences in local culture, I found that the people, at their core, were more alike than not.

Eventually, as a few more years went by, I did travel cross-country and visited many major cities. Again, I noticed many differences ... but I also noticed many similarities.

Today, I continue to travel all over the United States with little fear or trepidation. It is not much more difficult for me to visit a city taking a three-hour flight traveling nearly 2,000 miles as taking a three hour car trip to a city 200 miles away. The financial costs are somewhat higher, but the *time costs* are quite similar.

I do this today on a fairly regular basis because I visit and meet with business friends and associates at varying business-related events.

Prior to this, my contracting services were nationally available. Clients would hire me for individual weekly assignments. But occasionally, there would also be multi-week assignments. Regardless, I often took an airplane and traveled nationally on a fairly regular basis. Occasionally, I would be able to drive there.

As I traveled, I eventually created a network of relationships across the country. I often joke today that I know more people outside my city rather than within it. Although I do joke about it, it is also true.

But this is one of the benefits in attending business events, conferences, and seminars away from home. Nearly every person who attends such an event is away from the familiarity and responsibilities of home. As such, people often network and socialize together, and the relationships created often continue long after the event. In the age of the Internet, with email, discussion forums, and calling cards, it is easier than ever to keep in touch with people and maintain the network.

Today I view all cities with very different eyes. I appreciate and enjoy the local culture and uniqueness that each city offers. I also have great peace of mind knowing that most cities are not so foreign where I could not visit, live, invest, or do business there.

I see many people who value their so-called "stability" so much that they have become prisoners within their own communities. Most people do not travel much beyond where they live and where they work. Living-related activities, such as shopping and recreation, are also mostly within those areas.

It's not a problem that they prefer that; it is quite normal to want to have a "home base." What I see is that people refuse to leave their confines because it is "too far" or "too inconvenient." When I lived in Atlanta, people regularly spent up to two hours a day commuting back and forth to work and spending considerable time on the roads. Yet, some of those people would never fly out of the city to attend a seminar or some other business event that would help them in meeting contacts or learning from people who could give them the knowledge they need to set them financially and personally free.

People will spend thousands of dollars on vacations and travel thousands of miles away ... but they will not travel for things that can truly make a long-term difference in their lives! Does this make sense to you? It really doesn't to me.

I will often recommend someone to attend an out-of-state business seminar or conference. Do you know what the reply I usually receive is?

I hear: *"Isn't there anything closer?"* or *"When will the next class come to this area?"*

When I hear these comments, it often means that the person doesn't want to travel out of their comfort area ... or they are just simply lazy. In the age of relatively inexpensive airfares (provided you know how to plan ahead and know the basic rules to secure discounted fares), you can go nearly anywhere in the continental U.S. in less than an 8-hour workday. And unless you are flying coast to coast, you can travel to most places within half that time.

I have said for many years that, "The United States is my playground." What I mean by that is I am able and willing to travel anywhere in the United States for business reasons. Most people simply do business locally, but I do business nationally. More recently, I have begun to do some business internationally.

The problem I see with strictly adhering to local business is that it is too restrictive and narrow in this era of globalization and international business. Also doing business exclusively local makes you vulnerable to the downturns of the local economy.

Likewise, I see many tourist cities, such as those in Florida and Nevada, that are too dependent on business outside of the local economy. They are extremely vulnerable because the local economy can't support all of the tourist facilities and infrastructures. One of the reasons I left Florida was because the local economy was predominantly tourism-based ... therefore it was too dependent on and vulnerable to the outside economy.

I like cities that have a more cosmopolitan and diverse mixture of local industries. However, even with this, I continue to operate nationally and internationally.

An ex-coworker friend of mine commented to me a few years ago, "Matt, when you make decisions, you always like to have many options."

I replied, "Yes, I do. When I have different options, I have the freedom to choose the path best for my circumstances and me. When I have few or no options, there is little freedom and I am forced down a path."

Many people say that they have little freedom and few choices. I say that they have few opportunities and few choices because their playground is too small.

If people would only expand their playground, their choices and opportunities would expand.

People Don't Want to Move

One of the things I notice about people is that they like to stay within a familar community and they dislike changing it. I don't like change myself ... nor do I like a sense of isolation. However, what I dislike even more is being *stuck and trapped*.

It was a very challenging time when I moved from Orlando to Atlanta several years ago. I was moving to another state ... to a different class of city where I knew absolutely no one. It was very disruptive to my life, but I made that choice because I wanted the opportunities.

A few years later, I was once again compelled to move. It was more important for me to magnify the weight of my financial resources and increase my chances of my success rather than to not move and preserve my sense of familiarity.

It has been said that you can make money anywhere. You know what? I agree with that. But there are also economic and business conditions that are more favorable in some areas than others.

For example, I have visited various cities in California over the years. Some cities included Sacramento,

Santa Barbara, Los Angeles, San Francisco, and San Diego. I love the climate, scenery, entertainment, food, and all cultural diversity California offers.

Although I don't like to say "never," I can safely say that as a business and investing environment ... I find it to be one of the least favorable states to be in. The laws, regulations, and red tape to operate in California are beyond what I am willing to tolerate. As it turns out, my tolerance is relatively low.

In my view, there are too many places in the United States to live, invest, and do business in ... all of which are more pro-business and pro-investor than what California is.

I bring this up because many people live in California. Inevitably, beginning entrepreneurs and investors living in California realize the incredible amount of unnecessary obstacles they have to overcome ... and they become discouraged. They ask if there is anything they can do to make doing business easier there.

But I rarely respond to those people because most of the people won't like my answer.

My answer is to move elsewhere so that you don't have such a problem. Of course, people who live in California generally love living there and don't want to move. And who can blame them? However, it is a choice ... a personal choice. But you have to pay the price for living in California.

Again, I don't want to say it can't be done. It can! But I am a person that believes it is much easier to move and change yourself rather than try to change the local business laws and community.

Regarding the moving issue, I would like to offer an alternative view. There are immigrants (both legal and illegal) who are willing to risk their lives and personal well-being for the opportunity to work within the borders of a country that they are not literate or fluent in. These people also do not have access to the

Internet or long distance telephone calls because of the language barrier. *They literally try to cross oceans and deserts just to get where they need to be.*

I find it pitiful that people who have so many civic freedoms and who speak the English language, find it so difficult to rent a U-haul and find another place to move to! After all, in the age of the Internet, cell phones, and calling cards, it is easier than ever to keep in touch with family and friends ... no matter where they live in the country.

I don't think I will ever quite understand why people like to limit themselves so much.

Personal Faith

In the age of terrorism, we tend to think of political and military power. However, in the world of entrepreneurship, one of the most powerful forces is *the power of personal faith.* It is also a powerful force in the global world. After all, it is the power of faith that drives the various sects of religion.

I have chosen the word "faith" instead of "belief" because the word "faith" has multiple connotations ... and it has special meaning to each person.

One thing I have noticed regarding the issue of faith; there are many people who claim to have a strong faith in themselves and a Higher Power. However, I have seen a lot of those very same people who are scared to take a small risk to make changes or willingly stop doing something that is no longer fulfilling or working for them.

I recently read an online article on how more people are more discontent than ever with their jobs. While that may be informative, I am fairly certain that many of them will remain discontent because of their fear of change and the lack of faith in themselves.

I left the corporate world without anything lined up. I only had a very small nest egg, a couple of credit cards, and credit lines. It was not the minimum six months worth of income saved up that so many people recommend. It was my *faith* that allowed me to believe things would work out *if I did my part* in moving forward ... and looking and working for opportunity. But what really made this a bit scary was that I publicly told everyone that I wasn't going back to my old business.

I did this deliberately so that it would drive me to become successful in "going for it" ... *to be personally free.* So on one hand it was scarier than ever ... on the other hand, I knew it would serve me well going through the experience. Five years later, I understood the power of faith when it was again called upon. I believed that if I did my part, things would ultimately work out.

I would like to clarify here that when I said things would, "ultimately work out," it does not mean I would not encounter setbacks ... or even failure. In my mind, it simply meant that even if I were to go bankrupt, I would have to rebuild my financial life. Even with my worst-case scenario, I never thought that I would become some derelict wearing smelly, old clothes digging through garbage cans in dark alleys for food. That simply did not enter my mind.

I would also like to say that having faith does not mean being foolhardy, reckless, unethical, or irresponsible. It simply means that if you are reasonably intelligent and resourceful, and you are willing to do your part and be responsible for the results in your life, things will ultimately work out. Your sense of faith has to tell you that things always work out for the best.

Leap of Faith

In a scene from one of my favorite adventure movies, *"Indiana Jones and the Last Crusade"* (Harrison Ford as Indiana Jones and Sean Connery as Indiana Jones' father), Indiana's father is deliberately wounded by evil captors. Indiana is forced into a position to save his father's life ... and the only way to do so is to use his father's notes and successfully find the holy water that will restore his father's rapidly ebbing life.

However, there are many ancient booby traps that Indiana has to get through before getting to the holy water. In one particular trap, Indiana runs to the edge of a cliff and abruptly stops where he sees a deep chasm. Unfortunately, Indiana needs to cross this huge chasm in order to get the holy water. He realizes he cannot cross it by simply jumping across. It is simply too far away.

Indiana panics, but looks to his father's book of notes for clues to solve the puzzle. The notes show a drawing of a man walking on air across the chasm. Indiana is understandably very skeptical and agitated. He says to himself that this challenge is a leap of faith. So he looks across span of open air and then down into the deep chasm at what might be a fall to his death. But he also knows that his father will die if he doesn't muster up the faith to walk across.

Indiana then mentally prepares himself, closes his eyes, takes a breath, and lifts one leg to step into the chasm. Expecting to fall to his death as he takes the first step, he surprisingly discovers that his foot lands on an "invisible" bridge. Indiana discovers that the bridge was only invisible because it was camouflaged to look like the cliff walls.

He then quickly races across the bridge and finds the holy water to save his father's life.

The point of this story: there may be times in your life where you think you have done everything you reasonably can ... but it still looks risky. You may want to consider what your leap of faith might be and *when* you will take it.

In Indiana's case, he desperately needed to save his father within the next several minutes or he would die - so he was willing to do it. Yet, to others watching him, it would seem to be a rather foolish risk.

We occasionally encounter circumstances in our lives ... in business or personal relationships ... where we may be called upon to take what most people would consider a "foolish" risk. Only you can be the judge of whether it is worth it or not.

For me, anytime I feel I have done everything I can to prepare but still feel insecure of the outcome, I think of the movie "Indiana Jones and the Last Crusade" and that "Leap of Faith" scene.

The Winds of Change

One of the things I have noticed in today's society is the rapid pace of change. This rapid pace of change is embraced by some people and feared by others.

The pace of change is overwhelming for many people ... especially people who are accustomed to a time where there haven't been as many technological, social, and market changes.

There is a saying that younger people tend to adapt to change better than older people. As a generalization, I do believe that is true because older people tend to create habits that they feel comfortable with. It gives them a sense of security. But it also holds them back.

For example, one of the things I dislike changing is the time at which I get up in the morning (actually late morning ... truth be told). Also, I prefer to go straight to the computer and read the news before I go to brush and floss my teeth and wash my face. It isn't that there is any particular rationale to it ... I have just simply grown accustomed to it. Then when I have to deviate from that, I am able to do so ... but not without some personal discomfort. I don't like my morning routine changed!

There are also the kinds of changes that occur beyond our control:

- The newest styles become fashionable when you are comfortable with your clothes that have now gone out of style.

- Your favorite store has gone out of business or relocated.

- The neighborhood you live in has become run down.

- The music that has become cool actually annoys you and gives you a headache to listen to.

- The road you drive on is being repaved and you are redirected to another road.

The list is endless of all the changes that occur around us ... and we have to live with them.

Then there are fundamental changes that can potentially alter your lifestyle and well-being:

- The stock market crashes and there seems to be nowhere safe to invest your money.

- The local, regional, or national economy goes into a recession.

- A company downsizes, which in turn results in a layoff of 10,000 people.

- The skill sets you had that were so in demand five years ago are now obsolete.

- A company brings in new computers, machines, and equipment that automate all the jobs you used to do.

Do these sound familiar? These changes are very real to many people. And unfortunately ... most people do not know how to cope, nor can they see which way they should go when changes happen to them. They become confused, lost, and angry.

The reason I bring this up is because these changes often occur to those who are ignorant or simply in the dark - whether it is by choice or not. They are not tuned in to what I call the "winds of change."

They know the winds of change are blowing, but because they cannot see the wind or know which way it will blow, they refuse to believe that it will affect them.

Most people seem to have little experience or the willingness in finding the Winds of Change, much less figure out which direction it may blow. People like to talk about sailing, but most don't want to get into the boat. They don't want to get wet and they don't want to risk capsizing. That seems to be the nature of many.

The Winds of Change are too frightening for many people. They feel the force of the wind, but they cannot see it. They figure that because they cannot see the wind, they think or hope that this invisible force will go away. What these people fail to realize is that most of us have a boat to navigate. Being in denial that you are on a boat does not mean the winds will not affect you. The truth is *everyone* is riding a boat that can be capsized. It is all a matter of degree ... and time.

Invisible winds of change are very powerful ... and they are often unavoidable. It is all in how you respond to them. Most people refuse to ride the Winds of Change; they would rather try to anchor down and let the winds blow. The problem is most people's chains on those anchors are not that strong ... and they will eventually snap.

The Winds of Change (A Poem)

By Matthew Chan

*The Winds of Change is Nature's Force. You are the Captain of
your ship in the Sea of Life. How will you sail?*

*There are those who believe the Winds of Change move slowly
and has little force when it blows as a breeze.
There are those who believe the Winds of Change move
quickly and forcefully because it blows as a gale.
Then, there are those who simply believe the Winds of Change
do not exist because they cannot see the Winds of
Change blowing.*

*The Truth is:
The Winds of Change move both slowly and quickly.
The Winds of Change blow both as gently as a breeze or as
forcefully as a gale.
The Winds of Change blow continually ... even though you
cannot see it with your eyes.*

*Those who look for the Winds of Change will never see it
blow.
Those who daringly sail the Winds of Change will only feel
its flow.*

*Those who sail against the Winds of Change are carried to
the Lands of Confusion, Desperation, and Scarcity.
Those who sail with the Winds of Change are carried to the
Lands of Opportunity, Purpose, and Prosperity.*

*The Winds of Change is Nature's Force. You are the Captain
of your ship in the Sea of Life. How will you sail?*

Hurricane Parties

When I was a young teenager in Florida, I remember nearly every year from August to October there would be a lot of talk about hurricanes because it was after all the hurricane season. Of course, there would be hurricane-tracking coverage on television to find out where a hurricane would go. There was also a lot of coverage of past hurricanes, how much destruction had occurred, and the things that happened to people and what they experienced.

I remember hearing about "hurricane parties." When I heard that phrase, I did not exactly know what that meant. I thought to myself, "Why would anyone have a party in a hurricane?"

In all the news footage I saw, there was simply utter chaos and destruction as a result of a hurricane. It was pretty obvious to me that having a hurricane hit your city was extremely bad news. And if it hit ... there would be big problems.

I asked someone what a hurricane party was and he said that there were people who thought of hurricanes only as "bad storms." They would have a party in the exciting "bad storm" while everyone else was preparing for the worst by boarding things down or evacuating from the area.

What I did not mention earlier is that there were many hurricane parties that ended with people being killed. Today, you will still occasionally hear about people throwing a hurricane party.

In looking back, what I realized is that people in hurricane parties did not believe, or they chose to be in denial of, the power of the wind and rain. After all, how much harm could the wind cause? How much damage can water cause? After all, you can't really see the wind, and the water is normally this soft substance that comes from our faucets, right?

They are unable to comprehend how nature can create the gentle breeze of wind just as easily as it can also create the monster of a hurricane wind. Or taking that one step further, the soothing running water they feel in the shower could very well be the raging flood that drowns them in a hurricane.

They are unable to, or choose not to, recognize these distinctions ... and many people have paid for it with their lives in a hurricane party.

I still see people having hurricane parties today. The biggest economic hurricane party I saw was the Technology Stocks Rush from 1996 to 1999. It was one of the biggest in history.

Many people knew that stocks COULD go down ... but they chose to ignore it. People were rolling their retirement plans over and borrowing money so that they could get into the stock market. And as the hurricane became stronger and closer, the more people wanted to get into the party!

In the fall of 1999, I saw signs that a hurricane would soon wash everything away. One reason I knew a hurricane was coming was because I had fairly conservative mutual funds. These funds, which traditionally did not have any huge swings in past years, all of a sudden began swinging up and down in value (mutual funds by design are not supposed to swing up and down as much as regular stocks).

People who knew little about stocks started to quit their jobs to do day-trading. All of this seemed insane to me. Listening to the daily craze called the Stock Market News, I surmised a hurricane was coming ... and it was coming fast and hard. However, like everyone else, I did not have a magical crystal ball to tell me exactly *when* it would hit.

That winter, I knew it was time to start "boarding up my shop and evacuate," so I began to set things in motion to plan my escape. By the following month, I had already evacuated out of the stock market and had converted all of my mutual funds into cash. I then also announced my departure from the I.T. industry that same month ... and four weeks later I was out of the information technology business.

My intuition told me that when the Internet stocks crashed, there would be many technology companies that would go with them ... so I had to get out while the getting was good! Ironically, the times seemed to be great for everyone else. But for me, it was the calm before the storm. And I had to take advantage of it!

As you read this, there will probably be people that will fall into two camps. One group will say that I was just lucky. The other group will say that I was very astute. The truth is probably somewhere in between. It was not pure luck because I saw a number of uncomfortable events come to pass. And it was mind-blowing to me that the end came only three months later!

It was also a conscious choice for me to get out when I did for the very concerns I mentioned, and it was based on what I saw happening in the market and economy.

As I said, it was not entirely because I was so astute - because I did not have a magical crystal ball to predict the future. It turned out to be both luck and some insights of what was to come. I anticipated what was *likely* to happen, based on the most current information available to me. As it turned out, I made it out safely while many people I knew watched their savings and retirement plans get washed away.

The point of this story is not to publicly pat myself on the back, but to illustrate that there are hurricane parties going on in the world where people are often in denial or simply unable to see what is coming. You can choose to leave or you can choose to stay. You live with the consequences of your decision.

Seeing the Hurricane

As I mentioned earlier, I lived in Florida where I experienced many thunderstorms and hurricane watches. From the ground, there is little way of telling when a storm is coming. We cannot see very far from our limited perspective on the ground ... so we rely on reporters and meteorologists looking at radar and satellite photos, as well as other weather instruments to measure air pressure, air temperature, wind speeds, and other weather indicators. These people are *trained* to see storms, hurricanes, and other weather anomalies that most of us cannot until it's too late.

I now spend a lot of time training myself to look for weather indicators because I do not want an unseen economic hurricane to unexpectedly hit me.

Part of the reason why I was successful in attaining personal freedom was that there were certain things I saw coming. As such, I could change direction and plan accordingly. I have said that I do not recommend going "cold turkey" to embark on a mission of freedom. I prefer to advise people to do it at a slower pace so that they can reduce their risk while moving forward.

However, in my case, the sense of urgency was too great. The storm was coming. Figuratively speaking, I had no time to pack up everything I wanted before getting on the road. It was imperative I got on the road ... and I did!

Change is Inevitable

➤

When people ask me what I would consider to be the most important factor to my successes, I would have to say that it has been my ability to adapt and accept change in business and economic environments.

As I have said, most people inherently do not like change ... especially when it comes to their daily routines, their work, and where they live. People like variety and stimulation, but are generally resistant to fundamental and significant shifts in their professional, personal, and financial lives.

While I wish I could take full credit for my ability to adapt and accept change, I have to admit that I was mostly forced into it!

When I graduated from high school and entered the workforce full-time (while also attending college), I became aware of the wide array of choices I had as a young adult. I would often become confused because there were so many directions and choices I could take in my life.

Because I didn't know what I really wanted, I took the opposite approach. I looked at what I *didn't* like and what *did not* look promising.

I had an aptitude for science, math, and computers in school. Therefore, I elected to pursue electrical engineering as a major. While browsing through the college catalog, I noticed that the curriculum looked astoundingly similar to what I had already successfully studied.

Unfortunately, I underestimated the curriculum. I earned a very poor cumulative grade point average my very first semester, and was then swiftly placed on academic probation. This was quite disheartening for me ... high school was far easier! I soon discovered that I hated most of the courses I took for engineering. So in a desperate attempt to salvage my short and downward spiraling college career, I changed to Business to take what I considered to be much more practical and interesting courses.

While I did succeed the following semester in improving my grades to a stellar C average, it was not enough to offset the academic disaster I had caused in my first semester. After the second semester ... in completing my first year of college ... I was academically disqualified. This meant I was no longer able to attend the university.

Because I was still living at home and I knew how my mother valued my getting a college education, I hid this fact from her for many years (out of my own shame and embarrassment). She never understood why I changed to a community college ... but the reality was simply because I had no choice. The universities were not going to accept me, so the only way I would be able to get a college education would be to start over at a lower-level school.

During that summer, I worked full-time and had great fun doing it. I didn't have to think about school. However, it was inevitable that I would have to decide what I was going to do. I would either become a college dropout ... or find another way to go on. After much introspection and self-evaluation, I finally decided that I needed to adapt to the situation despite my humiliation and embarrassment.

In the mid 1980's, steps were being taken to cut back on many contract jobs in the defense industry. This meant that many engineers and other contract defense workers would be fired from their jobs. This fact really stuck in my mind. I decided to fully commit to the Business Administration curriculum. I didn't want to be an unwanted engineer that no one would hire.

Although I had done poorly the first two semesters from a grades point of view, I did in fact earn many credits despite my low grade-point average. This in turn meant that I only had to attend one more academic year to receive a two-year degree ... which could later be applied towards a four-year degree. In looking at the big picture, I realized that getting the degree was more important than worrying about my poor grade-point average. I couldn't go back and fix it ... I could only go forward and make the best out of what happened.

As it turned out, because I was working full-time, it took me much longer than a year to finish earning my credits to receive my two-year degree.

As I look back on all this, because I had done so poorly academically the first year, it actually freed me from worrying about graduating with honors, being valedictorian, or any of the other types of recognition that would normally reward me for doing so well academically. I wasn't as concerned about grades as much as simply getting through the classes with my degree. Although I got the occasional "A," I settled for B's and C's until I graduated.

Meanwhile, little did I know, a friend of mine had experienced a similar mishap and was also expelled from the university. He also had no choice but to retrench and attend the community college that I had also attended. Ironically, we both completed our two-year degrees the same year. Seven years after our high school graduation, we had both earned our four-year degrees.

What greatly separated us was that he received a degree in Engineering, while I received my degree in Business Administration. I had continued to aggressively pursue my professional career along with my degree ... so that when I did in fact graduate, I was already well entrenched into the corporate world.

My friend graduated into a nation with a glut of engineers in a time of recession, where he found few opportunities and openings. Although he was aware of the current events, he proceeded on because he did not want to change his course. He wanted to complete what he started. While that was commendable, he ultimately suffered because he refused to change his strategy.

When personal computing evolved into network computing, I sensed that there were changes afoot. In turn, I felt I needed to evolve with the next stage in the evolution of computing. Therefore I acquired industry certifications with leading vendors at a relatively early stage to capitalize on future opportunities of growth.

Years later, I began to hear talks of the "World Wide Web" and the "Internet." It was during that time when I began to learn about and familiarize myself with these new trends. I went on to become one of the first technical instructors in the country to use the Web to market my business and services.

Unfortunately, because I still had old ideas about business and money, I neglected to aggressively pursue the Internet in a much larger way. As a consequence, I never became an Internet millionaire when the opportunity presented itself. While I did not initially succeed at that time to become an Internet entrepreneur, I vowed that I would stay involved by becoming an aggressive user of the Internet, as well as a content provider.

As a side comment, I do think there will be a second Internet revolution … and this time I don't intend to miss it. How I will do that is a discussion for another time.

A simple book I recommend people read is, "Who Moved My Cheese?" by Spencer Johnson. There is only one certainty in the world of business, finance, and economics … *change*.

We must either flow with change or become an agent of change. I have chosen to do both. This book is part of that strategy. I am morphing myself to become an author. Simultaneously, I hope to inspire change and help create more entrepreneurs and investors.

If change is not something you are willing to accept, I would not recommend going into business or investing. It is the very nature of change that often allows the creation of wealth and money.

Wealth is often created during uptrends, and it is often transferred during downtrends. Money can be made during both up-trends *and* downtrends. However, the strategies are different. *We must change with the times.*

When I see young adults in their early to mid 20's, I see a lot of confusion and desperation. The latest news reports say that nearly half of all college graduates will not find a job. Unfortunately, no one has taught them how to create their own jobs and opportunities by becoming an entrepreneur.

The young adults see the world as being more complicated. To me, the world is not really more complicated ... because human nature remains relatively the same. However, our personal freedom and options are greater than ever before. Because schools and parents continue to perpetuate old ideas, young adults are confused in the adapting of those old ideas into our new world.

In effect, they realize something is amiss. They don't know what the problem is, but they know *something* is wrong. Those who have accepted change often become agents of change ... such as the Internet entrepreneurs, real estate developers/investors, financiers, businesses, and so on. *They profit immensely because they adapt well to change.*

Those that do not allow change to enter their lives get left behind. They cling to their jobs and pray that the economy never goes bad. But nevertheless, history has shown that change is inevitable.

One particular friend of mine feels that times are different because of the age of computers, software, etc. He believes that technology itself controls changes. But my opinion is that human nature will always prevail. *People drive technology ... technology does not drive people.*

A few years ago I also realized that the world was going to continue changing, and that my financial problems were a direct result of my actions. In order for me to change my situation, I needed to change myself, what I believed, and the way I did things. In effect, I needed to *reinvent* myself.

I assessed my strengths and weaknesses, as well as my core beliefs and assumptions. I then capitalized on those that worked in my favor, and got rid of those that didn't. I realized that I had to adopt new beliefs and ideas.

In a conversation with another friend, he told me that he didn't want to retrain in order to try new things. He said that my ideas would continue changing, and that I would jump from one thing to another. I thought about what he said, and I realized he was right. It bothered him that I had to continue changing. Yet, I felt that I had to. When I did, it usually worked out to my benefit ... where new opportunities would then open up.

I found it interesting that while he wanted financial security ... so did I! However, our approaches were vastly different. He needed the security *now*. In my view, the time when we need the most security is in our later years ... when our health and professional opportunities tend to deteriorate, but our responsibilities increase.

As a final note to this chapter, I would really like to add a sentiment that my own editor actually said to one of her other clients. I think it really adds to what I am trying to stress:

"Consider the seasons, trees, plant life, everything ... the way in which it constantly changes, grows, dies and is reborn once again. Constant change is needed in order for the Universe to thrive. Change is learning ... change is growth ... change is moving that one step further down your path."

6 | Personal Support Networks

Personal Support Networks

It is fairly common knowledge that we are all influenced by the people we associate with.

In our families, we have spouses, children, siblings, or parents who can and will influence us.

In seeking friendships, we tend to associate with people who have common social, professional, emotional, sexual, religious, or cultural interests.

Furthermore, within our professional relationships we tend to associate with people we serve, such as clients and customers, as well as with those that serve us ... such as service providers, suppliers, our alliance partners, or other people within our industry.

Much of this evolves over time, and we take it for granted because these relationships seem to "just happen." People come and go in our lives for various reasons. It's much like a revolving door in a hotel: people check-in for a while and then they checkout. It is an ongoing process.

One thing that became immediately clear to me years ago was that the personal journey I was about to embark on was going to be quite significant: not only was I going to leave the industry I was in, but I was also going to become a different type of entrepreneur; where it was not just for the money ... it was for the lifestyle.

As I announced my plans and started to set everything in motion that would ultimately lead to my departure, I could sense that the people around me were being affected. Unfortunately, I wish I could say that I was met with unequivocal support ... but alas ... it was quite the opposite.

Because I had earned a respectable living, position, and recognition over the last ten years in the information technology industry, almost *no one* could understand how I could walk away from the income, or why I would want to leave to begin with ... and they certainly questioned the validity and reality of creating streaming income and building income layers.

Although I had plenty of determination, inspiration, and emotional conviction, I still had my insecurities and fears about whether I made the right decision or whether I could actually accomplish what I set out to do. I don't think that it would come as a surprise that I wanted some moral support ... if at all possible.

Unfortunately ... I did not receive any. And this created some great distress for me. No matter what I said to anyone, it was met with resistance and with little or no support. To be fair, I realize that no one did it with the intention of hurting me; they did so with the good intentions of "helping" me. But it was not the help I wanted.

Suddenly, my professional contacts could no longer be my professional contacts because they had no idea what I was about to do ... nor did they have any interest. My friends, who so valued security, their jobs, benefits, degrees, titles, and positions, did not see the wisdom in walking away from it all to enter a world where your performance counted and not your credentials. Family members valued their perceived stability and security instead of the uncertainty and risk I was about to take.

In one fell swoop, I suddenly realized that I had no personal support network. In an emotional sense, I was suddenly all alone. There was no one I knew that I could consult with on informational issues, nor was there anyone I could count on for moral support.

Having been self-employed for those previous five years, I realized that I no longer wanted to do everything myself. It was simply too grueling and limiting to have my business endeavors limited to just me. I had no problems in starting a project myself; I just simply didn't want it to be where it would forever totally dependent on me.

What I realized was, for me to increase my chances of success, one of the first things I had to do was rebuild my personal support network from ground zero.

There were four areas I concentrated my efforts on:

1. New friendships with like-minded people - who did not necessarily have to understand what my business interests were, but did understand the paradigm I was working under.

2. New relationships with like-minded peers - who had the knowledge and expertise within the business areas I was about to enter, and also who I could consult and communicate with.

3. New teachers and mentors, who would be able to teach and guide me in new ideas, information, and techniques.

4. New business partnerships and alliances with like-minded people.

By focusing on synergy creation, I was able to develop relationships with the "right" types of people.

Kinship Network

I discovered during my early years as an entrepreneur that there were far more people who had planned to work in jobs until old age than there were people who wanted to work hard for their personal freedom.

Their need for certainty and security of a steady income, despite the fact that they would always be dependent on the whims of some employer, outweighed their desire to have autonomy and personal freedom.

Because of this, I often felt like I was alone in my quest for personal freedom. And while I would share my ideas, thoughts, and feelings on the matter, very few people could or would want to relate to it.

But then I also discovered that just because I had a friendship or acquaintance with someone, it did not necessarily mean we had a mutual *kinship*.

Because the desires and drives for personal freedom are so powerful, they are rooted at an emotional level. It is this understanding of these emotions that create a mutual sense of kinship. *"Yes, I know what you are talking about. I feel the same way. I feel your pain."*

Because the pursuit of personal freedom is more often an internal journey rather than external, having people around you who are supportive of your efforts and who can understand it can be very important during times of stress, disappointment, and setbacks.

As I realized that my journey to personal freedom was largely an internal (emotional) one, I found that associating with people of like-mindedness was very empowering, inspiring, and motivating.

A group of like-minded people to support one another is what I like to refer to as a *Kinship Network*. I coined this term to offer some different distinctions to familiar concepts.

For anyone wanting to undertake this journey to personal freedom, I highly recommend that you join or form a kinship network. These are people of like-mind, but may not necessarily be people of similar skills, abilities, and talents. *The importance of a kinship network is the like-mindedness.*

Finding people of like-mind can be quite challenging for people who choose to do it alone. To create a Kinship Network, I recommend the following:

- Seminars & Workshops

- Conferences & Conventions

- Online Discussion Forums

Of course, there are other ways to find a kinship network. But I found that when people speak and learn about similar interests together, it is much easier to cultivate a kinship network.

Mindshare Network

As I continued my journey for personal freedom, I did ultimately find many people of like-mindedness. I discovered that there were plenty ... especially when I attended a seminar, convention, or conference! There were often hundreds of people that shared my dream of personal freedom!

But as with many things in life ... you can also have too much of a good thing. After a while, I knew plenty of people who were on a similar path. In fact, most people I regularly associate with today and know me on a personal level are of like-mind. I do not have to consciously think of a kinship network because nearly everyone I choose to associate with on a regular basis are in fact of like-mind.

The next step I discovered was that I wanted and needed a *Mindshare Network*. I have coined this term to represent a group of people who associate with one another because they have complementary skill sets and expertise.

The idea behind a mindshare network was that I could never know everything about any given subject within my entrepreneurial and investment ventures, and I would inevitably need to get advice, feedback, guidance, or expertise from people whom I could reasonably trust.

People within my mindshare network tend to be people who are more knowledgeable than me in certain areas, who have similar abilities as mine but have a different view on things, and even those who are simply more successful than me ... and of whom I can consult with.

The point of a mindshare network is to have the ability to openly share information and expertise with one another without a feeling of threat and competition. Often, members of my mindshare network are in different parts of the country, or even outside of my country. So really, there is little concern of geographical competition.

Within the realm of the Internet, geography is often not a barrier to competition; I tend to find people who have different interests or niches to alleviate the competitive concern.

The power of a good mindshare network is that it can transcend your geographical location. With the availability of emails, online discussion forums, chat rooms, faxes, and calling cards, almost anyone living in today's world can be contacted fairly easily.

For example, one of my instrumental income layers comes from real estate. More specifically: single-family homes for lower middle-income families. Because real estate can be somewhat involved in many different aspects, such as financing, contracts, taxes, insurance, administration, management, and so forth, I have a mindshare network of people throughout the United States that I can consult with and ask their advice. These people are primarily active investors themselves, but I also have contacts that are attorneys, accountants, inspectors, agents, and so on that are crucial parts of my mindshare network.

I have said to some of my associates that I take great comfort in knowing that I can move anywhere within the United States, and in a short time confidently invest in real estate to create income layers for myself, my financial partners, and investors. Of course, that is simplistic and there are always small pieces of uncertainty and the unknown. But my point is, my mindshare network in the area of real estate is expansive and comprehensive enough that I can pick up the phone or email someone to get nearly all the answers I need.

In other cases, such as the Internet, my mindshare network consists of the companies I work with. Not one company knows *all* the answers. However, collectively they have most of the answers I could ever want.

Something that I recommend people *don't* get caught up on are the semantics of the mindshare network. People within your mindshare network need not specifically agree to such a title. If you call them and they are willing to talk to you and share their expertise and experience in a reliable and credible fashion, then they are a part of your mindshare network.

My business interests primarily lay within a few major areas: real estate, media publishing, and Internet projects. Within each area, I have different people that are a part of my mindshare network. And in each case, there is very little competitive concern. So in turn, I am able to tap into them when I feel the need to.

Support Network   ➤

There are essentially four types of support people in the realm of entrepreneurship. They are: teachers, peers, students, and mentors.

I find that each type of person is essential to continuing my personal and professional growth. Each type of person has a specific purpose and role, but there are also people who may simultaneously fulfill more than one role.

However, it is important to recognize what those types of people do for you.

Teachers   ➤

The first one is the easiest to understand: *the teacher*.

A teacher is a person who you learn or emulate from. They are the providers of information, expertise, and experience in a given subject or subjects.

A teacher may be someone you may or may not know personally. They can be a coach, mentor, professor, expert, author, or a seminar instructor.

As I mentioned earlier, most people think that when they leave college their education has ended. For many, their true "real-life" education has only just begun.

When I decided that I would change my life and work to become personally free, I realized that the teachers I had were not going to be the teachers for my future. The teachers I had were instructors in the area of networking technology; not teachers of investing, marketing, salesmanship, entrepreneurship, business, and finance.

I knew that in order for me to ultimately succeed in reaching my goals, I had to find new teachers. As much as I like to think that I am intelligent and well studied, deep down I realize that there is always more I can learn. I also know that it can be difficult ... especially as an adult who had established himself in a career for nearly ten years as an expert to suddenly become a student of other teachers.

I had to be willing to put my ego aside, to not be the center of attention, to not be an expert, and to be an unknown student once again. After all, students generally are not people who are the centers of attention. *Students give their teachers their attention*. Students spend their time, energy, and money to learn.

In order to find new teachers, I had to systematically decide what I needed to learn. Often, I did not have a specific skill set *per se* that I wanted to learn. I simply had a general idea of what I wanted to learn and I opened myself to it.

For example, when I set out to learn more about real estate investing, I had to be open to learning about financing, real estate law, contracts, marketing, and so forth. There were things that appealed to me, such as learning more of the legal aspects and creative financing, but then there were other things, such as learning to become a real estate agent, that I did not feel was useful for what I was trying to achieve.

Today, I am proud to say that I had many teachers ... and I continue to have many teachers; my list of teachers continues to evolve. As I learn and master new skills and ideas resulting in greater wisdom and knowledge, I phase out old teachers and actively find new ones. Some of my teachers have become my business allies ... some even friends.

My teachers are sometimes people I already know ... but often they are not. In fact, that is how I often meet new people and expand my network. At first, I seek them out as my teacher, and then eventually they become a peer, friend, or a business associate.

Although I have not reached old age, I am confident that I will continue to have teachers for as long as I am productive and alive.

There are people who say that they no longer have teachers. When I hear people say that, I know then that they either have become arrogant where they think they know everything, or they have become stagnant where they have chosen not to learn new things from others.

As we live on this world, there is always someone that can teach you something new. Because we are not omniscient, we cannot know about everything everywhere.

Because I have accepted that I will continually have different teachers in my life. The converse of that is that I will be a student in life ... for the rest of my life.

Students

Students are people who you pass your experience, knowledge, wisdom, skills, and knowledge onto. But students are not always people within classrooms. They can be your children, younger siblings, or simply a friend who is not as knowledgeable or experienced as you in a certain area.

As I said earlier, I have dedicated my life to be a life-long student. I am an avid learner, and I continuously enjoy and practice personal, professional, and spiritual growth.

Teachers I admire often profess to be life-long students themselves. I am guessing that they are wise and knowledgeable because they made an effort to learn so much for so many years.

Students play an important role in your life because the act of teaching requires clarity of thought and concept. It requires good communication skills. In effect, students allow the teacher to learn more intently because they not only have to learn the skill for themselves, but they are learning with the intent of passing it on.

I have to admit, that when I was a teacher of networking technology; there was a certain sense of pride, fulfillment, and recognition that came with it. Being a teacher required me to take on a leadership role. But I discovered something. *With the act of teaching a student, the teacher reinforces the lessons for themselves.* Also, by teaching, I got newer distinctions for myself because students would ask unexpected questions that I was then challenged to answer.

When I left technology training, I didn't think I would get back into teaching again. However, during the course of the last few years, as I gained successes in rebuilding my life, people became curious of how I did it and would ask. One of the reasons for this book is that it allows me to teach more people than what I can physically reach.

Although the student gains benefits by the act of listening and learning, the teacher *also* gains benefits of the learning through explanation and continued reinforcement.

In effect, if you choose to accept your role to be a student ... and perhaps a life-long student as I have, you will eventually have to find your own students to teach so that you may reap the learning benefits as a teacher.

Again, we generally think of students as being confined in classrooms. Although I have taught students in classrooms, I now consider some people I mentor as my students, and perhaps many readers of this book... such as yourself!

It is my hope that you are one of my students as you read this book. We may or may not ever meet. But the act of writing this book has forced me to make finer distinctions and clearly expand my thoughts of what I have already learned.

Peers

The next group of people in my personal support network is my *peers*. These peers are part of my kinship network, and sometimes also my mindshare network. These are people who you would generally consider to be "on your level" in terms of experience, expertise, and knowledge.

Although they are on the same level as you, they are essential for ongoing support. They are people who you may consider as friends and you have some commonalities with, yet there are enough complementary differences where it is still enjoyable and productive for both of you.

The interesting thing I have noticed about my peers is that because they often live a life of personal, professional, and spiritual growth, we learn and grow in different ways. Like cars on a highway, we are not necessarily in a race with another. However, we do pass each other in different lanes and different parts of the road at different times.

When this happens, I sometimes become their students and follow and learn from them. Other times, I become their teachers by leading and teaching. But because we are primarily on the same highway of life, despite the to's and fro's, we can still come together in social situations and simply be peers.

Remember: the journey for your personal freedom will put you in contact with many drivers in their own cars. But it is always the most fun when you drive and race together ... not against each other.

I have seen that people tend to associate more with their peers throughout their lives because they are people with whom they are most comfortable. Peers are also the most likely out of the three groups to be your friends ... mainly because of this comfort factor.

Virtual Teachers

Because ongoing learning was, and still continues to be, an essential part of my success, I often focused on finding the right people to come in contact with where I would form support networks.

However, there are other places where there is a vast wealth of knowledge ... where you can reach people who we could not normally otherwise reach. They may be people who are inaccessible, or they may even have already deceased. They have left their marks behind in books, videos, and audio recordings. We also have the wealth of information on the Internet, our public libraries, and bookstores.

Our libraries, bookstores, and the Internet collectively contain a huge warehouse of knowledge, experience, and wisdom!

As an entrepreneur, some of my business heroes include Sam Walton (Wal-Mart), Michael Dell (Dell Computers), Louis Gerstner (IBM), Bill Gates (Microsoft), Donald Trump, and Pierre Omidyar (eBay).

Each of these people I have listed are either deceased or inaccessible to me. For me to learn from them, in effect to become my virtual teacher, I read the books they have written. I also read books and articles other people write *about* them.

I read about them to not only study their business successes, but also to get a feel for what kind of person they are or were. I create in my mind that they are a teacher ... to the best of my ability ... in order to gain wisdom and experience from them.

In a sense, because I consider them a virtual teacher by reading their books, in a small sense I am also a part of their legacy. Although none of these people know me or anything about me ... I still consider myself their student.

Aside from books, I have virtual teachers from audio and video recordings. I often buy audio programs to listen to. Sometimes a professional reader reads them, but often I prefer those where the actual author speaks ... because I not only learn what they have to teach, but I get to hear their voice and experience in some small way what kind of person they are.

The nice thing about audio programs is that when I don't understand something or I need to relearn a subject, I have the luxury of replaying a section of tape or CD as many times as I need in order to understand it.

Although I enjoy reading, I also enjoy learning through audio because I can do it while traveling ... whether I am driving a car or riding in a plane. It makes it very time efficient.

Mentors

In this section, I would like to talk about a special type of person within your support network that do not clearly fall within the prior three categories of teacher, peer, or student. That person is the **mentor**. In many ways, mentors fulfill the role of each.

Mentors have different meanings for different people. An active mentor is someone whom you have a personal connection with and they take an active interest in you. It is easy to see the role they play as a teacher. However, they are also a peer in the sense that they have to relate to you as a fellow person. Furthermore, an active mentor becomes a student as a result of their teaching.

Active mentors are interested in the whole person ... not simply the subject matter. They mentor and provide guidance on the basis of your personality, goals, and personal characteristics. Mentors offer more than subject matter or technical knowledge ... they also provide *wisdom and experience*.

Good mentors provide mentorship with or without financial compensation, but I prefer mentorship that goes beyond financial compensation. Mentors are generally self-motivated and have a more personal need to give. However, because good mentors value their time, they will not mentor without some kind of exchange. Using financial compensation is only one way to find a mentor. I have often found that most people I would look to for mentorship are not interested in financial compensation at all. They are more interested in making a difference ... and they prefer the fulfillment that comes from it.

Mentoring requires personal time and energy - both of which are highly valued by a potential mentor. They value their time and generally do it on their terms ... so they may send conditions to qualify you. While they may be willing to mentor, they are not willing to waste their time on someone who does not listen or demonstrate intelligence, congruency, honor, commitment, and initiative.

They may mentor when they see potential in you. They may do it because they like you. They may do it to enhance a business or personal relationship. They may do it because you remind them of themselves. Or ... they may mentor you simply out of a sense of giving and contribution. Regardless of the reason, they mentor for reasons that are often beyond the obvious.

Part of my own personal journey was that I needed some guidance that went beyond technical knowledge. I wanted to gain wisdom from those that went before me. You see ... now I spend a lot of my time understanding and harnessing invisible and intangible forces. *Wisdom is one of those forces that can be gained from a mentor.*

What a mentor gives is their personal energy, information, experience, wisdom, insights, and most importantly ... their time. Each of these things should be treasured.

It's important to understand that most people who become mentors don't simply get out of bed one day and say to themselves, "I intend to become someone's mentor today." It just doesn't work that way.

A personal mentor is the one most people seek and perhaps the most challenging to find. Because many mentors don't often want financial compensation, it can be difficult to figure out what a mentor wants in a relationship.

To find a mentor, you must ask yourself why he or she would want to mentor you. If your answer is to say, "Because they have the time, money, or knowledge," you may be quite disappointed. Just because someone has the time, money, or knowledge it does not necessarily mean that they are obligated to mentor you. Nor does that really create the desire for them to mentor you. It simply is not that inspiring for a potential "mentoree" to take and not give anything back.

Many people want a mentor to receive what they can get, but the person seeking mentorship is often not prepared to give. These people are stingy. They listen to "conventional wisdom" that says you should not work for free.

What Are You Offering?

Many people who are unaccustomed to seeking out or working with mentors think that money is their highest priority in creating a relationship. That is because they place money of high value and they have a great need for it, and they automatically assume that the other person also has the same need for money. Sometimes that may be the case ... but other times it is not the case at all.

There are also people who think that they have little or no money ... that they have nothing to bring to the table. Again, that may be true in some cases. However, often it is not.

True mentors will give an objective and balanced opinion. They will tell you when you are doing well, and they will also tell you when you aren't! A good mentor will generally know things about you, which might include personal, financial, professional, and spiritual aspects of you.

A good mentor will not only have good analytical skills, but they will also have good intuitive skills. Mentors are advisors, teachers, and counselors. A good mentor is to be cherished and valued, and the relationship should be cultivated and nurtured.

Many beginning students are focused on what they can get from the mentor than what they can give in return. *Every mentor is different*. It is *your* job to learn more about the mentor and the type of person they are.

Mentors want to know that they are not wasting their time with you. They want to know that the knowledge, experience, and wisdom they pass on to you are being used and applied ... not ignored. The quickest way to lose a mentor is to give the mentor the impression that his advice is being ignored. After all, why would a mentor bother teaching a student or apprentice if he or she will not listen?

In dealing with my own mentors, I am always focused on giving them things that they cannot easily buy. I give them my time, attention, and positive reinforcement ... I show them that what they are saying and teaching to me is being heard and understood. I give my mentors exposure and bring them outside business when appropriate. I also give my mentors genuine and heartfelt opinions. I do not play the "yes man" or become a groupie. I am respectful, but I also treat them as a real person. I encourage my mentors to be their true selves in front of me. I assure them that even if I see their flaws and imperfections, I will still regard them as my mentors.

And if I disagree with a mentor, I do so in a way that lets them know that despite a disagreement, I still support the mentor and what he represents.

In order for a mentor to exist, there must be a student. Often, my mentors never even realize that they are my mentors. They become mentors by virtue of my being a good student and apprentice. A good apprentice spends a lot of time listening and reaffirming that he understands and will apply the all knowledge he receives.

There are people that continue to learn ... but yet never apply what they learn. There are few things more disappointing than having a failed student.

Secret Tips to Getting a Mentor

I have always found it relatively easy to find mentors in my life. However, I also learned at an early age that *wisdom* is *not* easy to find. There are a lot of smart people ... but there are not many *wise* people. But when you have wisdom on your side, life is much easier. Most mentors have some kind of wisdom we want.

Part of getting a mentor is to understand the type of person a potential mentor is. What do they like to talk about? What do they like to do? What foods do they like? Are they morning people or night people? Are they patient or impatient? Do they like public attention and admiration, or do they prefer to stay low key and subtle? The questions are endless. But the bottom line here is for you to get to know more about the mentor and their background.

I am going to reveal some of my best secrets to create a relationship with a potential mentor:

- *Work for free or do something of value for them.* Don't put conditions on it, but certainly express your desire to learn, get their insights, and share their experiences ... or whatever you want. This really goes against the grain for many people, but that is why it is easy for me to separate myself from others. It isn't because I am so good when I volunteer; it is often because so few are *willing* to volunteer.

  There is no guarantee that this will work, but you will certainly make an impression on them with your willingness to give on the possibility that you might spend time with them.

- *Do not be greedy and be respectful of their time.* Time is something that cannot be bought back. Once it's gone ... it's gone.

- *Do not be a groupie.* Give the proper respect ... but don't be patronizing.

Some of my mentors are fairly well known in certain circles. When you are reasonably well known or associated with someone well known, you are often subjected to a lot of attention and requests for your time.

Remember: you have to do something that will separate you from other people. The way to do that is to give a potential mentor something *they* value ... not something *you* value. What you value may not be of value to them!

Mentors in public view often appreciate public support in what they do. The best people to give support to are those who have not quite "hit the big time." They are on their way, they have successes, and they will likely ultimately succeed. But if you help speed up their journey with public support and endorsement ... they will certainly remember you.

You may also align what you do to what they do. Whatever their goals are ... support them! Find a way to donate or contribute to the cause. Find a way to enhance or amplify what they do to make them more effective.

It is important for you to find out what sort of value you can bring them ... not for them to come up with an idea for you to do.

Success in Auto Racing

In my very last job as an employee, I worked for a well-known company known for putting on stock car racing events.

During race time, nearly every employee was required to be either on-site or on-call. In my case, I was both. I would sometimes go out to the top of grandstands to get an aerial view of the race. The view I saw of the cars is not unlike some of the aerial shots of races I sometimes see on television.

I would watch these drivers race around the oval course in fixed patterns at speeds nearing 200 mph. If airplanes flew in the sky, like the cars drove around the course, I would say they flew in a formation flight pattern.

As I watched, several cars would be in formation ... speeding around the track. Like most auto races, accidents happen or they need maintenance ... and in turn those cars would break formation.

However, the cars that remained in formation often resulted in one or more cars lined up behind one another ... driving in a close, tailgate fashion. Quite often there would be two lead cars ... with one closely behind the other.

I remembered asking my boss, "Why are all the cars driving in formation like that? Why are they tailing each other? I thought that each driver's goal was to be the lead car."

"These cars are not tailing," he replied. "They are drafting one another."

"Drafting?" I asked, feeling rather puzzled. "What is that?"

"Drafting is an aerodynamic phenomenon where the displacement of air from the first car creates a vacuum for the second car," he smiled.

Interested, I then asked, "What is the point of that?" Taking me to one side, he then further explained:

"Drafting allows the first car to have a more efficient displacement of air, thus conserving fuel. Because the second car is so close to the first car, it dampens the effect of the vacuum that would normally slow the first car. The second car also conserves fuel because it is pulled along by the vacuum created by the first car."

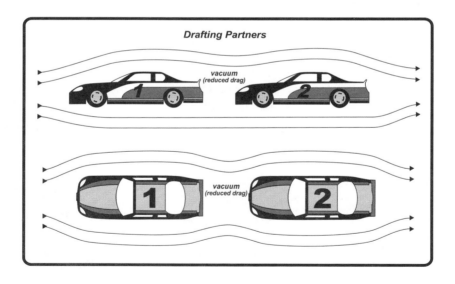

Intrigued by the concept, I asked, "So, although the front car and the rear car are competing against each other, they are also helping each other?"

"That's right," he nodded and smiled. "They cooperate with each other in the beginning of the race by drafting so that they can lose the rest of the cars. And when they have gained a good amount of distance away from the other competitors, they will then compete with each other to attempt to win the race."

In my mind, I thought, "Wow! What a concept."

Based on our conversation, I surmised that for a car to go solo (which the driver could decide to at any given moment), the price the driver would have to pay was expending more fuel to overcome the greater drag a solo car would experience going on his own than if he had a drafting partner.

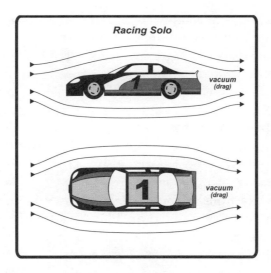

Like stock car racing, I decided if I was going to be in the race, I had better look for drafting partners because the cost of racing solo was too great for me.

Based on my limited sports knowledge, I had always thought that a sport was about brute competition where opponents played to win. They won by NOT cooperating with each other. I saw this in boxing, football, basketball, tennis, and other sports. The whole point was often to upset and unbalance the opponents early to eventually win the game.

Meanwhile, in NASCAR racing, opponents cooperated with one another to help them win the race. Understanding this concept of cooperation with opponents and competitors to win the larger game was an important lesson for me.

In later years, as I studied successful businesses, I found this to be especially true in the personal computer hardware and software industry.

Prior to the IBM PC, there were no "universal" standards for computers. All computers were proprietary. Computer hardware made by one manufacturer would not work on another computer made by another. Likewise, software produced for one brand of computer would not work for another.

The personal computer industry exploded into a multi-billion dollar industry because having "universal" hardware standards produced a "greater good." IBM, Dell, Hewlett-Packard, and other smaller manufacturers are competitors today in that each company produces personal computers to sell to customers. However, they have also chosen to cooperate by supporting the PC standard and not creating a totally proprietary PC. The overall personal computer industry continues to grow by this "co-opetition" (competition within cooperation).

For example, **Microsoft Windows** is very close to being a universal standard on PCs. And while there is a lot of debate whether it is in fact a superior operating system, the undisputable fact is that the overall PC software industry has grown immensely by its competitors *cooperating* with one another ... in agreeing to develop programs, games, utilities, and applications to be run under Microsoft Windows.

To the untrained person, they see everything as black and white ... in total absolutes. They believe that competitors must hurt each other, never be friendly to one another, and that they can never work together.

In my view, that is very limited thinking ... and it truly limits your options.

In school and college, a lot of emphasis was placed on technical, vocational, and professional skills. And while I do think they are important, I also feel that business relationship skills are just as important.

Today, when I approach people I don't know but who are interested in creating a business relationship, I often take what I call a "second-car drafting" approach. I focus on how I can help the "first car" win or finish their race (figuratively speaking) … whatever that might be. I am willing to let the other person be the "lead car." I know that if we can create a symbiotic relationship, such as NASCAR drivers do with drafting, I will also receive the benefits of being pulled along as the "second car."

I'm certain that by this point some of you out there are thinking, "He believes in riding on someone's coattail." To that, I will say that is not true and totally inaccurate.

"Riding someone's coattail" is simply getting behind the person and being pulled (or dragged) along and reaping the benefits and rewards with *no contribution*.

In drafting, both the first and second car **are** making contributions to the overall drafting effect. The reality is that although the first car creates a vacuum, the vacuum is insufficient to completely pull the entire mass of the second car. The driver in the second car must be willing to

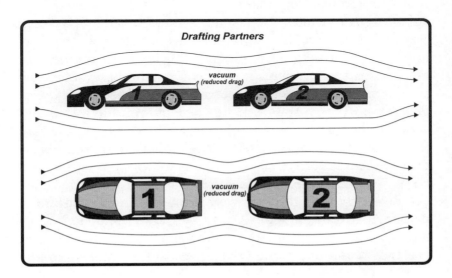

also use his fuel to take advantage of the draft created by the first car.

So, in my view, if you are the second car and using your own fuel (making contributions) to help the first car finish or win the race ... then you are drafting. If you are the second car and not using any fuel (making little or no contributions), then you would rightfully be accused of riding someone's coattail.

I would like to point out that when you seek drafting relationships, you don't say it as such to people who are not familiar with the term. You will simply get strange looks. The goal is to be of service and to offer something meaningful and of value to the person to whom you want to draft with.

As I mentioned before, I find that successful people do not want money given to them directly. If they do, it is to fund projects or investments ... not a charity handout. In a similar vein, people welcome referrals or efforts to create more business for them ... not simply a charitable money handout like I mentioned. They want more business they can earn.

I have often found that people need help in achieving greater recognition or more opportunities to meet new people so that they can meet their business needs.

Again, I would like to emphasize that this is not an exact science. Part of successful drafting in business is finding out what is truly important for the driver in the first car.

As a driver on the racetrack of entrepreneurship, if you intend to use the drafting concept, you have to know when to be the first car and when to be the second car. But there are no "set" and "exact" rules for this ... there are only guidelines.

For example, if I sense that public recognition and the need to be in the forefront is important to the other person, I will often volunteer to be the "second car" ... as long as there is an understanding that we intend to finish the race together.

If I sense that someone needs financial, emotional, or moral support where they simply need help in the race, I will ask permission to be the lead car and invite them to be the second car and draft me … as long as they are committed to finishing the race with me.

In the racetrack of life, it is often not important to finish as the lead car. Oftentimes it is more than good enough to just finish the race. After all, it is sad but true that so many people will never even get into the race car to even drive, much less finish the race.

Different people have different needs. I merely adjust my positioning depending on what I sense and what is said to me.

Because of this very powerful and effective concept of drafting, I rarely do business or invest alone. I have found that is far easier and quicker to get where I want and achieve my goals by creating drafting relationships with people rather than to try to be a solo driver.

I firmly believe that my ability to more quickly create income layers for myself, as well as the personal freedom I have today, are both results of my active pursuit of drafting relationships.

People to Avoid

As I have said, personal freedom is just as much about time freedom … as well as monetary freedom. Part of the time freedom is not only to decide who you will spend time with, but also deciding on who NOT to spend your time with.

The best analogy I can give is something that nearly everyone can either relate to or have seen people they know go through. For better or for worse (no pun intended), marriages break up everyday through separation or divorce. Yet while society prefers that marriages remain intact, the reality of it is that divorces occur … and quite frankly sometimes it happens for the best.

Sometimes it is because of severe circumstances, other times it is just from a mere lack of compatibility or chemistry. When the couple separates and they become single again, generally there is a feeling of sadness and remorse. But as they say, you should move on ... and often it is best to move on separately. It does not mean that there has to be hatred, dislike, or some other extreme negative emotion ... but unfortunately for some people, sometimes it is there.

I occasionally think back to my high school years and the people whom I associated with or considered as friends. I am no longer associated with anyone I knew in high school. It's not for any reason in particular ... I guess like many other people, we just grew and moved apart in our lives.

I also look back at my past employers and the people who I worked with. For the most part, I enjoyed my jobs and the people I worked with. I sometimes fondly reminisce during quiet moments when I feel nostalgic ... but I do not wish to go back! I will occasionally run into an old co-worker and we will be friendly, but other than that there are very few similarities or bonds between us. Once again I see ... we have grown apart.

I bring all this up because as you go forth and meet new people and create new relationships, you may find yourself in an uncomfortable situation with the older relationships. The old friendships and relationships that were once so pleasant and fulfilling may suddenly become unpleasant and empty. When the personal or business relationship becomes unpleasant, empty, and no longer fulfilling, not too much can be served by "hanging on." When these transitions and changes happen, you do not have to be ugly, spiteful, or have animosity ... you just have to simply let it go and move on.

The reality is this: I have encountered insecure, skeptical, negative, paranoid, small-minded, miserly cynics that have conspiracy theories in their minds. And while they may be law-abiding citizens, no one wants to be around someone like that. Their distasteful energies have a great impact on us ... and after just one visit with someone like that ... you can guarantee that you will feel rather negative yourself.

People tend to enjoy being around intelligent, charismatic, friendly, confident, generous, open-minded optimists that believe the world is their oyster with all the pearls for their taking. And while that may sound a bit fantastical ... maybe even a bit hokey ... deep down most of us enjoy and appreciate those kinds of people.

The problem is I find that these particular people prefer to associate themselves with similar types of people. They generally avoid skepticism, negativity, paranoia, and cynicism in their lives. And so they should!

A good example I can give is when you go to a lively party ... where you tend to perk up and be happier than what you originally were. But when you go to a funeral, you tend to be more somber ... even if you don't want to be. People affect other people ... people's attitudes will affect other people's attitudes.

To summarize: relationships will always change and evolve. People will come into your life, and while some may stay, others will leave only a short time later. Sometimes it is their choice; but other times you have to make the choice yourself. For me, making the hard choices of leaving certain relationships behind allowed for me to open and greet new ones. It is all part of the process.

Dart Throwers

In the previous section, I talked about people in your life that you should avoid and not have in your life if you want to fully pursue your goal of personal freedom.

There is a special type of person that works in a subtle way: the dart thrower.

Dart throwers are people who look to pierce and test the validity of the plans you create, the actions you take, and the ideas you believe in. The darts they use are their critical words and the piercing questions they ask. On one hand, dart throwers can be good for you because they can force you to be clear and certain that the course you plan to take is a good, solid one. They can force you to think about issues you did not consider or perhaps have overlooked.

On the other hand, dart throwers can be very destructive ... especially in the early stages of a new venture, plan, and simply a new way of life. This often happens when a solid mental, emotional, and spiritual foundation has not yet been established. Their intent is to subtly undermine what you are doing by creating additional doubt, insecurity, and uncertainty within yourself.

These dart throwers are especially damaging and have long-term effects because the darts they throw do not often harm you in an overt, direct way, and they are ongoing ... which in turn has a cumulatively negative effect.

In the beginning, I began nurturing my entrepreneurial spirit by attempting to start various side-businesses. Some of those businesses included a comic book shop, CD music store, laserdisc movie mail order, a computer repair service, computer consulting, and so forth. Some never left the idea stages. Others I did manage to get a business license, business cards, and even a couple of customers.

In each of those attempts, I clearly remember all the dart throwers in those scenarios. Looking back, I remember them telling me all the reasons why my idea would not work and how it could not be done. Of course, this was done in a subtle way ... but nevertheless still left a rather negative impact.

Despite all this, I did manage to finally launch and sustain a profitable self-employed business.

I now often chuckle to myself at how little I knew back then with all the false starts. Nevertheless, I ended up succeeding because of the all the practice I had in starting up. And each time I became better and smarter despite the dart throwers.

To determine whether a dart thrower is serving or stifling your best interests, you have to look to the person: their background, lifestyle, priorities, and achievements in their lives. If the person throwing the darts has come from a traditional path of a college education, working hard as a full time employee in a job they dislike and plan on retiring on Social Security and old-fashioned savings at age 65, I would probably say that these people would not be very helpful. Fundamentally, these types of people are dependent on others for the outcome of their lives and have very rarely, if ever, ventured out to try something new.

These dart throwers talk a lot ... but they have done and tried very little.

I have had other dart throwers who were entrepreneurial or investors themselves who understood the nature of risk versus reward. They knew the importance of time in relation to money, had proactive management over their lives, and were generally high achievers. I have found that these types of dart throwers provide good insights that you may not have. In fact, they can also help your position ... because part of their dart throwing includes offering support, ideas, and possible solutions. They come from a place of, "How can you best make it happen the most successful way you can?"

However, if you are intent on creating something new or never done before, even those dart throwers can at times be detrimental to what you are trying to do.

I thoroughly encourage you to become conscious of the dart throwers in your life.

7 | Business Networks

Business & Investment Networks

      During most of my years in the corporate world, I often functioned independently from other people. Although I participated in informal networks as a way to meet business contacts, it was not instrumental as an income-producing activity.

      When I exchanged direct labor for direct pay, the amount of time I put in largely determined the pay I received. Furthermore, if something had to be done ... well ... I had to take care of it. In fact, I had to take care of nearly everything.

      When I decided to work towards my own personal freedom, I realized that if I was going to produce income layers, I had to make the decision that I was *not* going to do it alone ... *right from the very beginning*. Just like I mentioned in the previous chapter, there was no way I could know everything about any subject, nor could I expertly learn how to do every task.

      In other words, I knew I would begin this journey alone, but I would ultimately have to grow my business by working with others in alliances and partnerships. I would have to be willing to spread my talents and wealth in order to attract people to my cause.

Thanks to the Internet, I became an active participant in various online discussion forums. This in turn set the stage for actual meetings (in person) as I traveled throughout the country to different seminars, conventions, and other industry events. I then leveraged that into building my own network of people through a community-based website.

I expanded the scope of my online business activities by combining my network with other people who I thought would produce the synergy I was seeking.

Because I had chosen to pursue real estate investing as one means of creating income layers, I simultaneously began expanding my network by bringing on a co-management partner. As my co-management partner took on more of the direct responsibilities, it allowed me to continue expanding the core I built. Working together, both of us formed the core of our local investment network and our own property management company. I also cultivated relationships with several real estate investors across the United States ... who also became crucial parts of my own mindshare network.

Along the way, I built a few more income layers by utilizing **eBay** as a method for marketing, as well as a method of worldwide distribution and sales.

By balancing all of these activities, I was able to create my own personal freedom - which ultimately allowed me the time to write the book you now hold in your hands.

In the last few paragraphs, I have given a quick overview of the disparate business networks that were combined or re-synergized during the last few years. All of this now allows me the freedom and opportunities I have today.

That is the power of pursuing a course of creating your own business network. Additionally, an investment network is extremely powerful, and it allows you the expertise, manpower, and investment capital that you could not easily accumulate by yourself.

Business Networks

In my own journey, I chose to create and assemble my own business network through my personal efforts. Because of my background and expertise in information technology, I chose to utilize the Internet as a key method for first creating a kinship network ... which then in turn ultimately lead to my personal mindshare network and online business networks.

However, I would like to point out that while I did create my own business networks (which in turned allowed me to create several income layers), there are *many* options open to you that already exist.

The Internet itself is one worldwide network. Yet, within the Internet there are many business *sub-networks*. For example, one very popular business sub-network is that of **eBay**. I highly recommend this particular sub-network for beginning entrepreneurs. It's a sub-network that involves several million members ... whose mutual sole purpose is to come together to trade goods and services. It is easy to get in and out of.

Contrary to popular belief, **eBay** is *not* about going to Goodwill stores, the Salvation Army, flea markets, or garage sales to sell used merchandise. And while some people do this, it is the difficult way to create income layers with eBay. I offer products that are not widely available as part of my strategy.

First and foremost, **eBay** is an online community, as well as representation of a large market of willing buyers and sellers. Like any online community or marketplace, success is determined by tapping into the invisible and intangible forces within, while also creating a system that will allow you to build a consistent income layer.

Obviously, I did not create the **eBay** business network; I only chose to participate *within* it.

An example of an Internet-based business network I created is a website called ***The MasterMind Forums*** (***www.mastermindforums.com***). It began very humbly, where its original purpose was for me to create my own kinship network. However, its success allowed me to create a business network in itself ... and it also helped to create my own personal mindshare network.

Another popular and powerful business network is the *franchise*. McDonald's, Burger King, Holiday Inns, Radisson Hotels, Subway Shops, Mailboxes, Etc., AAMCO Transmission, and many other popular companies are actually franchises that allow entrepreneurs and investors to participate and work within that network. The system has been created ... but it does require high amounts of capital or financing for entry. If you have access to that kind of capital or financing, this can be a tremendous opportunity in creating large sums of streaming income.

Franchises carry a large amount of national, and sometimes even international, credibility; as well as name recognition and goodwill among consumers. The franchise system you buy into can give you nearly instant credibility... but it will cost you. For most people starting out, the capital and financing required to buy into a franchise is a significant barrier of entry.

Another business network that I consider rather suitable for beginning entrepreneurs is a *network marketing company* ... and there are many of them. I see network marketing companies as a mini-franchise system where the barrier of entry is low and the cost to buy into the system is relatively inexpensive.

While I am not personally involved with any network marketing companies, I know some reputable people who are involved with them. The asset a beginning entrepreneur has to build is a network of resellers within the mini-franchise system. You simultaneously build your reseller network, as well as provide services and products to customers. One aspect that I like about network marketing companies is that much of the order fulfillment and servicing is done by a third-party ... whereby you can focus on growing the business instead of the infrastructure.

However, the challenge of working within a network marketing company is learning to not only sell, but also to nurture, coach, and inspire people within the network. As in other businesses, finding customers and cultivating and growing the business relationship and network are a few important keys to success.

Like I said, the good thing about **eBay**, network marketing companies, and other Internet-based business networks, is that the cost of entry is relatively low ... and you are connected to others of like-mind. Your success is highly dependent upon your willingness to be creative, to persevere, and to put in an amount of "sweat equity."

Other business networks include *dealerships, distributorships, reseller programs, licensing programs*, and *affiliate programs* that exist both in the physical as well as the online world.

The beauty of business networks is that you can choose to play both sides of the game. You can choose to participate within one or several business networks, or you can create your own business networks. For example, the cover of this book boldly advertises the corresponding website to this book, *www.theintrepidway.com*. The intention is to create another online community of like-minded people that you and I can associate, benefit and create synergy from.

A nice benefit of working within a business network is in getting away from being a sole proprietor where you have to do everything and everything depends on you. You create synergy and other intangible benefits by working with others.

Income Layer Investments

When I first began on my journey towards personal freedom, part of my asset base included holdings in mutual funds. As I educated myself more and saw the increasing volatility, I knew that I would eventually be faced with a decision. For over ten years I had slowly but regularly made contributions to both my investment and retirement accounts through automatic withdrawals. I simply did what I was taught to do many years earlier.

However, what I was taught to do became increasingly unsettling ... given what I had seen coming and also what I knew I could do. From what I could see, the risk was becoming higher with the increasing volatility ... and I would have very little control. After all, my mutual funds were determined by what the stock market said ... not what I had to say. In fact, I had little or no say at all as to what would happen with the money I invested. I simply had to pray that the stock market thought that my funds were valuable.

Simultaneously, I began exploring investment alternatives ... such as real estate. For many years I had been tainted by the idea of real estate because of the whole "landlording thing." I heard and saw smaller landlords literally toil over their properties, and while these properties did provide some cash flow, I also saw the downside.

Despite my tainted view of real estate, I knew that it was a massive field full of diversity and specialties. Furthermore, because my family had owned a few properties, I had the advantage of being exposed to the idea and reality of real estate and cash flow, as well as many of the legal aspects and contracts involved. Despite my negative bias, I also saw that my background could lend itself to possible success. I simply had to explore the various options out there.

I learned of and saw people buying or referring ("bird-dogging") distressed properties at low prices ... and then reselling them to renovators ("rehabbers") or other investors for a higher price. This practice is often called wholesaling or "flipping properties."

This never appealed to me much. In my eyes, it was not really the type of investing that generated the income layers I wanted. In fact, it wasn't really investing at all ... it was just another self-employed job. It was too active for my taste, and I saw people doing it who could never really stop. The problem was when these people stopped working and producing ... the income would come to a dead halt. The old adage, "you are only as good as your last deal," kept rolling in my mind.

I explored buying foreclosures on the courthouse steps, but I didn't have the capital base or financial resources to outright buy foreclosure properties at auctions in order to resell them. Even moreso, I was not too keen on the idea of trying to directly compete for these properties with bidders who were clearly more equipped in both capital and expertise than what I was.

I once again thought about conventional landlording and property rentals, but because I was working alone, I didn't necessarily want to take on something too management intensive.

What I was left with was a concept that most appealed to me and my situation: *Lease-Optioning Property*. This was a blend of me being a landlord without all the management responsibilities normally associated with being a conventional landlord, but it also allowed me the benefit of creating a source of streaming income.

From a technical and legal standpoint, I had the advantages of landlord-tenant laws to quickly evict problematic tenant/buyers, but also had the benefits of being a bank ... where I mostly collected payments.

For example:

In buying a property, I would buy lower, middle-class, 3-bedroom single family homes that blue-collar people tend to live in (within the $50,000 to $70,000 range), with anywhere between a 5% to 10% down payment.

I would then advertise the property in the local newspapers with *"owner financing,"* a brief description, and a phone number. Needless to say, I would always receive many calls. In fact, that is why I had a second phone line with a dedicated answering machine that had more information on the house (i.e. the "down payment," the monthly payment, and directions to the house). I would also tell them to drive there to visit the house for more information.

The fact of the matter was I knew from personal experience that there were plenty of "look and see" types. These types of people are those that are "window-shopping" from the comforts of their homes with their telephones. But you see ... I was only interested in people who were serious about buying a house.

The "look and see" types could get information they needed without burning me out with repetitive questions, and the serious types would go out to the property and look at it.

At the property, I had informational sheets in bright neon paper posted to the front door or windows. I also had *"Owner Financing"* signs on the property, which included my office telephone number.

It was at this point that I would then be willing to speak to potential tenants/buyers on the phone. Why? *Because they had actually seen the property.* The people who called never had the opportunity to call my office number because I would deliberately get them to see the property. In my mind, if they chose not to view the property, then they were not serious enough to begin with.

Sometimes it would be relatively quick: within one month of advertising, it would be "sold." Other times it would take much longer ... like three months. To provide some sense of scale, the average selling time, DOM (known as Days On Market), for selling property in my area is approximately four months. In more populated and denser parts of the country, it can take less than one month, while within smaller and rural areas it can be up to a year before the property is "sold."

But once a tenant/buyer decided that they had the "down payment" and could afford the monthly payment, it was simply a matter of meeting at the local Burger King to "close the deal" to collect the money and sign the agreements.

Once this was completed, I had created a brand new income layer for myself. That income layer came about because of the lease-option contract I had created. Because of the little system I created of screening and redirecting people, it required relatively little of my time. I could actually spend my time working on other things.

I would like to point out that in some cases, I probably could have sold some properties a little more quickly had I done the personal touch with each call. But in the *Intrepid Way* of doing things, time efficiency and management is of paramount importance. In my experience, properties tend to move at their own pace. You can help things along, but the overall local market still largely influences it. I found it was more efficient to continue producing new income layers and cultivate new opportunities instead of spending all of my energy on any one particular property.

For those of you who would like to see a sample transaction, the numbers are listed below.

"BUY"

Fair Market Value: **$60,000**   **30-year Finance @ 7% interest**

Purchase Price: $55,000   Mortgage Pymt: $329.00
(-) 10% Down: $ 5,500   Taxes & Insurance: $ 95.00

= 90% Finance: $49,500   Total P.I.T.I.: $424.00

**Our Holding Costs
(2 months)**

P.I.T.I.: $ 848.00
Marketing: $ 300.00

Total Holding: $1,148.00

"SELL"

"Owner-Financing" with Lease-Option

Resale Price: $65,000   Our Buyer's Pymt: $625.00
(-) Upfront Money: $ 2,200

= Refinance Price: $62,800

Contract Equity Position: $13,300.00
Total Cash Investment: $ 6,648.00
Net Cash Investment: $ 4,448.00

Net Cash flow: $201.00/month
Annual cash flow: $ 2,412.00

Our Cash-on-Cash Returns: 54.2%

Better returns than savings accounts, mutual funds, and most stocks!

By implementing this lease-option concept:

- You become a bank by collecting a "upfront money" and you finance the purchase of the house.

- A greater sense of commitment for the tenant/buyer that they are buying ... not just renting ... a house.

- You recover some or all of your initial cash investment with the upfront money.

- You are able to withstand vacancies better because you will ultimately receive some or all of the money lost to vacancy through the upfront money.

- Nearly no maintenance or repair expenses because they are generally willing to buy "as is" and take on nearly all the responsibilities normally associated with home ownership.

- The monthly payments are above market rents because people buying are willing to pay more than those who are renting.

- In the event of default, the eviction process is far more efficient and less costly than a foreclosure.

- Because you are leasing to your "tenants" with the option to buy, you receive tax benefits as if you were doing a conventional rental.

- And most importantly, the returns are spectacular and you have an excellent income layer!

As I said, my focus was on creating excellent returns and solid income layers. There are people who want to ultimately "own" the property in thirty-years. While there is some merit to that approach, it is a slow and sometimes painful one. For me, ownership is overrated ... especially when it comes down to property. Many sophisticated investors don't try to outrightly own most properties. But this is because the cash needed to outrightly own a property is often not worth what that money could be doing elsewhere.

In fact, I don't think anyone has to look too far in regards to finding the truth about home ownership. Very few people stay in one property for thirty years. They continue to move … and for most people, they upgrade when they move. So even if they roll equity from one property to another, they never really get that close to paying it off because of those upgrades. Don't forget that this does NOT count the home equity loans or credit lines that those people have taken out.

However, don't misunderstand me. I'm not opposed to outrightly owning property if one is inclined to do it for their own security and peace of mind. For me, it simply isn't good use of money when I know I can use it or invest it to create more income layers.

My view is that even a paid-off property requires income layers to support it. There are homeowner's association fees, property taxes, insurance, lawn service, property repairs, and maintenance.

When it comes to properties that produce income layers, it isn't important that I outrightly own it. What *is* important is that it continues be a good source of streaming income, and that it produces a good return for any money I put in.

Investment Networks

What I have shown you is simply a broad overview of what I do to produce income layers as part of my investment portfolio. And while I have several properties that I have management or ownership interest that produce income layers for me, I have friends that span the country (and even overseas) who are far more successful at it than what I am. In fact, they have 50, 100, 200, 300 properties that have taken the strategy of "buy on terms" or "resell on terms," and they have all generated a tremendous amount of wealth for themselves.

I bring this up because most people who try to invest in property try to do it alone. It can be done and done successfully ... but as I pointed out earlier, I have seen people who have tried to invest alone and it becomes a very difficult challenge from a time standpoint. While they may keep 100% of the holdings and returns, the portfolio they have created also traps them. They end up having another full-time job. Furthermore, the more properties they acquire, the more trapped they become. *This is not the vision or lifestyle of the Intrepid Way.*

Pretty soon, they start looking like a high-paid person who cannot get away from their business because they are unwilling to let go.

When I began investing ... I began alone. I did not have all the contacts I did today, nor did I have the support or investment network I have now. Although I began alone, my plan was to expand outwards to work with others who had expertise, experience, and who wanted to be part of a team. I wanted to associate with people who understood the power of synergy and abundance ... not someone who felt that they had to have 100% of everything.

Part of the long-term success in creating income layers, whether in business or investing, is that:

I do not invest alone!

If I look outside of real estate, I find that it rather difficult to find successful individual stock traders or day-traders. They exist ... but they are quite rare. However, what I do see are successful investment firms. But these firms ... these are the organizations that invest as *a team*.

Even larger successful real estate investors like Donald Trump and Sam Zell do not invest alone. These men have an incredible team around them. They may get the exposure and credit as being investment leaders ... but they do not invest alone.

For example, members of my local investment network include a management partner, real estate attorney, title researcher, real estate agent, mortgage broker, landscaper, repairmen, investors, and local bank contacts. I actively seek to continue expanding my investment network because I do not believe in investing alone. I want to continue adding, improving, and expanding the quality of my income layers, while also simultaneously maintaining a good amount of personal freedom and flexibility of time.

Outside local investment networks, there is the *national investment network*. I am a part of a larger investment network, which I participate in, as well as a national investment network I have cultivated myself.

The point of my involvement and participation within a national investment network is not necessarily to invest together (although it is a valid alternative), but it is the power of having access to other investors who are outside your area. They bring in an outside perspective and expertise that is not easily found in your local area. Sometimes there is a competitive nature within the same local market that would preclude you from being too involved with other local investors.

I take great comfort in knowing that I can draw upon the expertise of a national network with only a phone call or email. It gives me great security to know that these talented investors are also a part of my team from afar. I support them ... and they support me.

With the advent of the Internet, it's easier than ever to be a part of an investment network ... for expertise as well investment partners. For example, a person who is living in a "hot" or expensive area like California, which is tenant-friendly and *not* investor-friendly, could invest in more income layer friendly areas ... such as where I am located in the states of Georgia and Alabama - where property is relatively inexpensive, stable, plentiful ... and the laws are investor-friendly.

As it turns out, our property management firm dominates the owner-finance market of my local area and I am extremely happy about this.

My friends with their own investment networks tend to operate in a similar fashion as I do ... in that we work with investors in a *straightforward way*. We tell them BOTH the *bad* as well as the *good*. And some of them, like myself, operate in a local environment where they either dominate the owner-finance market or they have a significant presence in their marketplace.

To those friends, I am grateful for their continued support. As mentioned: I support them ... they support me. *That* is the power of an investment network.

I would like to point out that this goes beyond the investment club where the concept of "clubs" is physical attendance. Having an investment network means having the ability of working, supporting, and investing together, as well as receiving all the benefits without necessarily meeting at some club.

Investments Do Involve Risk

My bias in investing gravitates towards real estate and the housing sector. The reason for this is because in good times and bad, people will always need a place to live. As an intangible force, the emotional need for owning and living in a stable home is high. As a general rule, real estate is much less volatile than stocks, and residential real estate is less volatile than commercial real estate. Coupled with favorable landlord and tax laws and a great support team, residential real estate is, in my opinion, low risk for many investors. In fact, the risk is so low that people can actually depend and live off of the cash flow. Having an income layer from a savings account may be secure, but it is generally very small.

Like businesses, investments do have risks. However, the risk in real estate investments is not necessarily the loss of value ... unlike stocks. *It is the vacancy factor and cash flow factor.* Vacancies not only mean that you lose your income layer, but you have to subsidize the investment with a monthly payment until it becomes occupied again.

However, with good planning and management, those vacancies become less significant.

I derive my income layers from both business and investments for a reason. Businesses provide me the income layers and liquidity that bankers find attractive ... but it can be more volatile.

Investments give me the asset base that is attractive to other investors. It gives me control of what I do with my excess money from business. Personally, it also provides a more stable source of income with less direct effort.

In the foreseeable future, I have very little inclination to put any money into the stock markets because of the sheer lack of control.

Conclusion

This chapter is not meant to teach you all the intricacies of business and investing, but it is meant to show you the concept and power of utilizing business and investment networks to create income layers and personal freedom *the Intrepid Way*.

If you wish to learn more about the way my company creates income layers with real estate and understanding lease-options from an investor point of view, I recommend you visit ***www.turnkeyinvesting.com***.

It is not about doing things alone ... it is about creating synergy with others in networks. Creating my own business and investment network has been instrumental to my success in creating my income layers. It gives me the leverage I need to accomplish results that I could not have easily done alone.

8 | **Education & Learning**

How Fast Do You Learn?

Today, more than ever, your educational habits and ideas will determine your ability to create and maintain your long-term personal freedom. Remember, it is one thing to attain personal freedom, it is another thing to maintain it.

The following is what I focus on when I look to develop new knowledge and new skills.

- What I choose to learn.

- How fast I learn it.

- How quickly I can apply it.

- Evaluate my results.

This then becomes an ongoing cycle for me.

Part of the ongoing learning process is simply keeping up with what is going on in the world. In past years, it wasn't critical that you knew what happened on a national level … much less on a global scale.

However, because of globalization and the impact other countries have upon each other, I have found it necessary to at least keep a pulse on what is happening ... both nationally and globally.

Therefore, as part of my daily routine, I scan through CNN.com and MSNBC.com to get the latest news. They do a great job consolidating the national and world news into an easy-to-read format, which I can then choose to read.

Following the general news sites, I then move on to other websites of personal interest, such as financial sites that have my bank and credit accounts so that I can look over my financial status and see what payments have come in, or my merchant sites so that I can monitor the status of my sales.

This becomes a very routine but essential part of my ongoing educational process: just simply knowing what is going on in the news and marketplace.

The Marketplace

Ongoing education is very important in the *Intrepid Way* lifestyle of living and working. It provides the tools and leverage you need to create the results you want and need. It becomes much easier when it is part of your daily routine.

Aside from the news, I also check the marketplace to see what sells and what doesn't ... what's hot and what's not. The marketplace is a great place to learn new ideas and concepts. This is one reason why I read so many books on real companies and why they are successful. I also read the news of those companies. I am looking for trends and shifts in the marketplace. What do consumers want to buy? What do people sell?

It does not mean I will necessarily do anything about what I learn and discover. However, what it does allow me to do is prepare for sudden changes (such as economic hurricanes) that could make a negative impact me ... or even prepare for unexpected opportunities.

It is much like the analogy where the United States invests into our military and police forces to protect our freedoms by ensuring that no persons or country can forcibly take it away. But the military and police forces are not sufficient without having good intelligence capabilities for information. We also continue to pay taxes to **maintain** that freedom.

As an entrepreneur and investor, knowing what is going on in the marketplace is the intelligence I need to maintain my personal freedom.

Learning Styles

As I come to the close of this book, I would like to share a few insights about learning styles I gained along the way in "schooling" myself.

The discussion of learning styles is actually one subject of an entire book ... so I want to share with you my simple view of the various learning styles. This is important because we all learn in different ways.

The learning styles are:

- Reading

- Listening

- Watching

- Interactive Learning

- Practicing

Out of the list, I think the most important is *reading*. The reason for that is because most of the knowledge in the world is overwhelmingly stored in text format; whether it is a book, magazine, newspaper, microfilm, electronic file, or pages on the Internet. Without acquiring some proficiency, efficiency, and a habit of reading, it will be extremely challenging to move forward.

Listening to audiotapes, CD's, MP3's, or streaming audio files is an effective supplement to the learning process. There are more audio options now than ever because of the relatively inexpensive costs in producing mass audio media. Listening is effective for many people because it is sometimes more time-efficient than reading. It is not uncommon for people today to listen to audio recordings during travel, such as while driving a car or flying in an airplane. Sometimes, you can also play it in the background while doing other things at home.

Watching videos on tape, DVD, or streaming videos is also becoming yet another way of learning. Videos offer the added dimension of sight to audio so that you can learn by both watching and listening. However, the downside to video is that it requires more focus and concentration. Also, video is not yet as portable and the selections for video learning is far fewer than that for reading and listening.

Interactive learning actually engages the student. It is most often associated with a classroom or seminar setting, where there is some interaction with fellow students and the instructor. However, with the advancement of technology, it is possible to learn interactively through the computer ... with the Internet or software, or both!

Finally ... we have practicing. This is learning where you actually *do it*. In fact, there are many things that must ultimately be learned by doing, and not by reading about, listening to, or watching it. A prime example is driving. You can prepare by reading, listening, and watching others drive, but ultimately you have to drive yourself. It is the same with using a computer on the Internet. You can read about it, hear about it, and watch it being done, but ultimately you have to click the mouse and type on the keyboard to truly learn it.

I have seen many people who try to learn by jumping directly into doing it – without having some degree of preparation from the other learning methods. However, I have discovered that this can be an extremely painful way to learn.

As you pursue learning, it is important that you are made aware of your preferences of learning styles. However, keep in mind that each has its place in the overall learning process.

Because the bulk of knowledge is in text format, you will have to adopt reading to a large degree into your learning curriculum.

For knowledge-based learning, where you are learning theory, concepts, and ideas, reading, listening, and interactive learning will probably be the most effective.

For skills and experience-based learning, where you are trying to learn how to do something new, you will have the preparation and then the doing stages. The preparation can be the reading, listening, watching, and interactive learning ... and then you actually have to practice it by doing it.

In pursuing learning, I attempt to mix everything together to make a "learning stew." The purpose is for time efficiency, cost effectiveness, reinforcement and cross-pollination.

For example, I learned I could not attend every seminar I would be interested in. It was not always practical from a time or cost standpoint. However, I would then find the next best alternative by purchasing an audio or video recording of a previous seminar. If that wouldn't be practical, then I would buy the book, manual, or course.

I am actually quite generous with my book budget because I find that books often cost far less than seminars. Besides ... I can use books over and over again! However, there is a downside: much can be lost in written format by the distillation process.

For example, despite my best efforts to convey my thoughts in writing this book, it cannot substitute all the things I could or want to say if you were to have a conversation or be in a classroom with me.

And although I like seminars and conferences, I have to rely on my notes, manuals, and memory to capture a part of what I learned and experienced. The learning comes from meeting and interacting with people. The learning goes beyond any book or audio recording.

I do find that audio recordings are a good middle ground between simply reading books and attending every seminar and conference. You can pick up the subtleties by listening, but of course you are listening to a past event. There are no interactions and benefits of networking.

As you can see, each way has its own pros and cons. But I encourage you to utilize each method of learning to its fullest benefit.

Then once you are on your path of learning ... you will already be well on your way towards your goal of personal freedom and wealth. You will have reached your goal ... *The Intrepid Way.*

In Conclusion

Very early in this project, I realized I had more to say than I could practically fit into one book. There are so many other stories in my life that I wanted to tell to illustrate the many lessons learned over the years. If I had tried to pack everything I wanted into one book, then I probably would never have finished.

The challenge in writing a book such as this is that I continue to get new distinctions from new experiences. I also meet new people and encounter new situations. I found that each time some new event happened to me, I would instinctively want to run to my manuscript and change something.

But having worked in the software industry, I learned that you have to know when to stop adding new things into any given project otherwise it will never be completed. I had to be reasonably clear in my mind what absolutely had to be in the first book and what could come later.

As I write this and prepare to go to print, there have been so much in the news I wish I could comment on. But, that has to wait until another day.

One thing I don't like is a drawn out ending, so I will simply say what I need to say and let you go.

The Intrepid Way as I have defined it is a lifestyle. It is a way of living and working. It is a compilation of ideas, distinctions, advice, and personal truths as I see them. Some pieces may work for you wonderfully, other pieces may not.

Each of you have to decide for yourself what you will take in and what you won't. The beauty of this is that you get to choose what you want to adopt and believe. You have ultimately responsibility for your own life and no one else.

I would like to think that I have many more years of learning, experience, and wisdom to gain. This book represents a snapshot of what I have learned thus far. Will my views change in the future? Perhaps. Perhaps not. I cannot say definitively. After all, I am still growing and maturing. I will continue to do so until the day I die. The only thing I can say for sure is that what I have written up to now is true for me and the philosophy I live by.

There are still many things I want to accomplish in my life. With personal freedom, I have many options to choose from and many roads to explore. I fully intend to do so on a global level. I invite you to join me. As I continue forward, I plan on incorporating new distinctions, ideas, and experiences into future books.

I would like to invite you back so I can report to you what I accomplished and didn't accomplish, what I succeeded at and what I failed at. As a lifetime student, I will continue to push myself to learn and to continue to improve myself. I have no plans to simply "retire", do nothing, and wither away. It is no longer just about the money. It is about what I can accomplish in my lifetime.

I thank you for committing the time to read this book. I hope it has made some difference in your life as my writing and publishing this book has.

Do not be a stranger. Come back and visit. I would love to meet you.

Until next time … I salute you.

Matthew S. Chan

──── FREE AUDIO PROGRAM! ────

As a special bonus for reading this book, I invite you to download and listen to the special follow up Audio Program. I offer additional commentary and insights as supplemental material to the book.

It is my way of thanking you for making the commitment to life change and personal growth. You can get this FREE downloadable audio program by visiting:

http://www.theintrepidway.com/audiopart1

Acknowledgements

John Burley, for your friendship and opening your world family to me. It has been said we both would have been fine if we never met. I agree. But I look at the synergy we created together the last few years and I am awestruck. I thank you for your generosity and loyalty. And most especially for being Intrepid enough to be first on MMF. I could not have done it without you. You have made a huge difference in my life.

Wes Weaver, for being the courageous young man that you are. You are my business partner and you are my friend. You are wise beyond your years. The Intrepid Way could not have happened without your insights into things I could not see. Your belief and trust in me along with your hard work and patience has allowed me to create the personal freedom I needed to take things to the next level. I thank you for being in the drivers seat of the second car. The race has become more exciting drafting together.

Keith Cunningham, for being such an incredibly powerful and spectacular teacher. The knowledge and inspiration you have instilled in me and others continue to resonate forward like tidal waves in an ocean. You have provided keys to so many vaults to so many people. The insights you gave to my personal and business life will always be treasured. I salute you for making me a better man. And yes, I will use the butcher knife.

Cindy Chapin, for your nurturing compassion and being my confidante. I treasure our conversations and our time together. Your willingness to be straight with me at all times keeps me grounded. I thank you for being an anchor for me during these times of uncertainty where I am breaking new ground. Knowing that you will be at my side brings me great confidence in what I do.

Stephanie Olsen, for your friendship and going out of your way to work with me. Your support, both publicly and privately, mean much more than you can know. I look forward to growing our friendship to the new possibilities we both dream of.

Melita Hunt, for being the spitfire that you are and opening the doors that allowed Van and I to work together. I hope you will continue in your dream project that I know will impact the lives of the world's children.

Van Tharp, for your lessons in investing psychology. I am proud to help you extend your reach further into the world to share your wisdom and make a difference in others.

Joe Arlt, Jerry & Lisa Hoganson, Marleen Geyen, Bill Gordon, Damion Lupo, Troy Arment, Dean Edelson, John & Debbie McCants, Bryan Fergus, Steve Dover, Adrian Oakman, Felicity Heffernan, Brad Simmons, Chad Watson, Mike & Gina Hinds, Shawn Whetten, Gil Barden, Jim Sheils, Craig Chandler, Tony Edward, and Hymer. I am honored to have served with you as my Bootcamp brothers and sisters-in-arms with the General. May we continue to learn and grow wise from our experiences so that we continue to make a difference in others ...

P.J. Zwart, I appreciate our growing friendship despite the ocean between us. Doing business and investing together has been such a pleasure. Thank you for your trust in me.

Gina Redmond and Sue Holmes, both of you are the unsung heroines. You make possible for so many of us to do what we do. I thank you for your tireless support and making my business life easier.

Christi Williams, Marah Boyeson, Will and Mariko Brooks, Darby Totten, Ryan Stewart, Paolo Bruno, Beverly Weaver, and Jeff Trant, for being such great friends and being continually interested in what I do in this world. I appreciate the moral support you have given me to do bigger things in my life; to accomplish a larger life mission by allowing me to step up and become all I want to be.

➤ Acknowledgements

Roy & Gina Chambers for inviting me into your home those many years ago and looking after me like I was your son. I thank you for having the ability to pierce my shell and reach my heart. If I have that ability today to do it within others, it is because you showed me the way during my Journey through one of the Crossroads of my life and ultimately seeing larger Horizons for myself and others.

And of course to my family which includes my mother, my father, and my sister.

My mother, who I credit most for giving me the determination, strength of will and self-reliance to reach my past, present and future accomplishments. It is my greatest wealth and her greatest gift to me. I take great comfort in knowing that no one can ever take that away from me for as long as I live.

My father, for being a good listener and always having the highest confidence in me in whatever outrageous goals I have pursued. To have someone believe in you is one of the greatest gifts anyone can receive.

To my younger sister, Jennifer, who has had to overcome many unexpected things in life. You will achieve the personal freedom you seek if you continue to stay the course.

There are so many people that I have encountered that have impacted my life. It is practically impossible for me to list and remember each person. If I did not mention you, I trust you know what good things you brought into my life.

The Creative Team

→

The author often receives the sole recognition and credit for the finished book. People think the author did all the work. Nothing can be further from the truth. For nearly a year, I struggled to finish this book on my own. Then, I followed my own lessons and formed a creative team.

First, I want to give special recognition to my editor, Lisa Nash, for giving her nurturing energy to my book project. If the words flowed smoothly, it is because Lisa came onboard to help on this project. Lisa, I thank you for the work that you do. As the editor of my very first book, you will forever hold a special place in my life.

Second, I want to recognize my cover designer, Joanne Waser, for creating and transforming the cover of The Intrepid Way into such a stunning, eye-catching piece of artwork. Her incredible sense of creativity and flair was magical to watch as she took my descriptions and gave them visual life. For that, I will always be grateful.

Third, I want to recognize my graphic artist, Tara Andrysiak, for her creativity, patience, and providing the graphics and the initial concepts for the layout of the book.

Finally, I want to recognize my typesetter and desktop publisher, Katina Colbert, for beautifully and masterfully putting together all the scattered pieces of this book together on such short notice. Her incredible dedication, diligence, and hard work on this book helped make possible a timely release of this book. I will never forget the late night blitzes with bleary eyes it took to finish this project. I thank you.

To the four members of the creative team, I salute you for helping me launch the beginning of what I hope to be an impactful book series.

➤ *Acknowledgements*

I recommend each of these talented individuals. You can contact them at:

Lisa Nash
Editor
Free Spirit Literary
Rhifain213@yahoo.com

Joanne Waser
Cover Designer / Graphic Artist
JOW Graphics
www.jowgraphics.com

Katina Colbert
Typesetter & Layout
tmassa@juno.com

Tara Andrysiak
Graphic Artist
Mediawave Creative Solutions
www.mediawavecreative.com

The Intrepid Way

About the Author

Matthew S. Chan is the author of "The Intrepid Way", a self-improvement/lifestyle book that teaches the lessons of entrepreneurship, personal finance, and business to people who want to leave the confines of the corporate world.

After spending ten years in the daily grind of corporate life making significant contributions to his employers, Matthew escaped to become a successful entrepreneur at the age of 29. His business interests continue to take him across the U.S. where he frequently meets new people.

Matthew's entrepreneurial drive began to manifest itself while working in corporate positions in operations, supervision, accounting, and information systems management in companies ranging from small privately-owned companies to a billion-dollar conglomerate.

Matthew's business experience includes working within the hospitality, entertainment, medical insurance, sporting event, and information technology industries.

Along with working on new book projects and expanding his personal network, Matthew continues to oversee on a "part-time" basis, the management of his Internet businesses and his growing real estate portfolio for himself and his investment partners.

Matthew continues to enjoy the personal freedom of spending time working only on projects and with people he likes. And in his "spare time", Matthew enjoys eating dim sum, watching movies, taking cruise vacations, traveling to new places, and sleeping late.

Matthew's educational background includes a Bachelor of Science in Business Administration from University of Central Florida, and a Masters of Business Administration from Webster University.

Recommended Resources

Books I recommend to expand your mind and business knowledge:

"The Perfect Store" by Adam Cohen
Brief: How eBay became the successful company it is today.

"Sam Walton: Made in America" by Sam Walton
Brief: How the founder created Wal-Mart in his own words.

"Who Says Elephants Can't Dance?" by Louis Gerstner
Brief: How the ex-CEO turned a dying IBM around in the 1990's

"God Wants You to be Rich" by Paul Zane Pilzer
Brief: The global abundance not studied in the conventional economics of scarcity

"The Lexus and the Olive Tree" by Thomas Friedman
Brief: The impact of globalization

"Built to Last" by James Collins and Jerry Porras
Brief: What makes companies continue to endure

"The Luck Factor" by Dr. Richard Wiseman
Brief: A British research answers the question: Is luck truly random or something you create in your life?

Websites I recommend you visit on a regular basis:

CNN - cnn.com
Brief: Daily news in a concise, easy-to-read format

MSNBC - msnbc.com
Brief: Daily news in a concise, easy-to-read format

New York Times – nytimes.com
Brief: Daily news in a concise, easy-to-read format

eBay – ebay.com
Brief: Part of the new economy created by the company of the same name.

Amazon.com – amazon.com
Brief: Part of the new economy created by the company of the same name

Recommended Educational Programs

John Burley's Level 5 Advanced Investing Bootcamp

I highly recommend John Burley's Investing Bootcamp which focuses largely on single-family home, real estate investing. It is suitable for both the beginning investor as well as the experienced investor.

What makes this program powerful, is that in addition to a group of very knowledgeable speakers and instructors, it is staffed by two dozen experienced real estate investors and real estate entrepreneurs from around the world. It has the highest ratio of staff-to-student I have seen anywhere. There is approximately one staff member/instructor for every five students.

John has a superb instructional team and outstanding staff support. In fact, the program is so inspirational and powerful, successful graduates volunteer to come back to help John teach and support his students twice a year.

It is not just a great educational program, it is a great life experience!

You can find out more about John and his Bootcamp at: *www.johnburley.com*.

Let them know I recommended John's program to you.

Keith Cunningham's Mentoring Program for Entrepreneurs

I highly recommend Keith Cunningham's Mentoring Program because it is a powerful but highly personal program for beginning and experienced entrepreneurs. With a limit of 25 students per session, this program provides entrepreneurial education and mentoring support to a group of students for an entire year.

Keith comes from a background on Wall Street and corporate turnarounds and is truly an entrepreneur's teacher. After all, I wonder how many of his students will come in having done more than a $1 billion in business deals as Keith has. His qualifications are unmatched.

What makes Keith's Mentoring Program special is that it is highly personal which requires a high level of student commitment and group involvement. You cannot hide in this program. It is about learning the skills you need to accomplish the goals you set for yourself. And once you do so, you will be held accountable to action.

If you are a beginning or established entrepreneur, this program is for you.

It is not only a great educational program, it is a great life experience!

You can find out more about Keith and his Mentoring Program at: *www.keystothevault.com*.

Let them know I recommended Keith's program to you.

Coming in Spring 2004!

The
Intrepid
Way™ - Uncut!

Hear The Intrepid Way
the way it was meant to...

If you think the book was unconventional and controversial, wait until you hear the audio version.

This is not a reading of the book. It is the audio recording of author Matthew Chan speaking to a live audience of the principles and ideas of The Intrepid Way in a very direct manner.

He will reveal more about his own personal journey of entrepreneurship and personal freedom not covered in the book.

This audio recording of the live talk on The Intrepid Way will enhance, reinforce, and go beyond the ideas and lessons covered in the book.

Because of its content, this will not be available in any bookstore. It can only be ordered directly from *www.theintrepidway.com*.

As a special bonus, you will hear Matthew preview topics that will be written and included in Matthew's upcoming book, The Intrepid Way – Part II!

Coming in Summer 2004!

The
Intrepid
Way™ *- Part II*

The Intrepid Way was just the beginning.

The Intrepid Way was an introduction to a different philosophy of working and living in these turbulent times.

The basic formula was:

Personal Freedom = Monetary Freedom + Time Freedom

Matthew shared the true story of how after 10 years of corporate life, he escaped the daily grind of corporate life and being an employee, to become first an entrepreneur and later an investor.

He explained some of the basic concepts, ideas and thoughts he implemented that ultimately resulted in creating the personal freedom he enjoys today.

However, there is more.... Much more that could not fit into one book.

The true story and lessons continue in The Intrepid Way - Part II.

If you enjoyed the ideas and stories within The Intrepid Way, then prepare yourself....

The Intrepid Way - Part II will further reveal Matthew's experiences and insights during his entrepreneurial journey to create and build personal freedom for himself.

As a bonus, Matthew will also reveal some of the things he studies to anticipate, not predict, changes of the future.

Visit *www.theintrepidway.com* for the latest updates on the upcoming book!

The *Intrepid Way*™ Connection

Want to discuss the principles of The Intrepid Way?

If you enjoyed the stories and ideas of The Intrepid Way and want to discuss and share your thoughts with other people, visit The Intrepid Way Connection, our online community.

Within The Intrepid Way Connection, you will find like-minded people openly share their thoughts, ask and answer questions of how living and working The Intrepid Way can benefit their lives.

Here you can form kinship and mindshare networks with other people to accelerate your journey to personal freedom. You can brainstorm with other people the best ways to create income layers best suited for yourself.

The possibilities are limitless when you have like-minded people come together on this online community.

Be part of The Intrepid Way Connection.

Visit ***www.theintrepidway.com***.

The
Intrepid
Way™
LIVE!

You can bring The Intrepid Way – Live! to your city. Author Matthew Chan will occasionally make personal appearances to teach to groups of people to share his information, insights, and vision.

If you are interested in having Matthew present the principles of The Intrepid Way to a live audience in your city, you can contact him at:

http://www.theintrepidway.com/liveevent

Coming Soon!

www.turnkeyinvesting.com

We want to hear your Success Stories!

If The Intrepid Way has been helpful to you, we would like to hear your personal success story. Your success story could be included in the next book of The Intrepid Way Series! Share your story with the world how The Intrepid Way positively impacted your life and made a difference to others.

If your personal success story is selected for inclusion in the next book, you will be eligible to receive a FREE autographed copy of the next book and have 30 minutes of telephone discussion time with author, Matthew Chan.

Please email your success story to
success@theintrepidway.com
or visit
http://www.theintrepidway.com/success
for more information.